New

Product

Forecasting

ONE WEEK LOAN

New Product Forecasting

An Applied Approach

Kenneth B. Kahn

Foreword by Martin Joseph and Alec Finney

M.E.Sharpe
Armonk, New York
London, England

Library of Congress Cataloging-in-Publication Data

Kahn, Kenneth B.
   New product forecasting : an applied approach / by Kenneth B. Kahn.
      p. cm.
Includes bibliographical references and index.
ISBN 0-7656-1609-2 (cloth : alk. paper) — ISBN 0-7656-1610-6 (pbk. : alk. paper)
   1. New products—Forecasting—Methodology. 2. Product management. I. Title.

HF5415.153.K33 2006
658.5'75—dc22   2006005481

Printed in the United States of America

The paper used in this publication meets the minimum requirements of
American National Standard for Information Sciences
Permanence of Paper for Printed Library Materials,
ANSI Z 39.48-1984.

∞

| BM (c) | 10 | 9 | 8 | 7 | 6 | 5 | 4 | 3 | 2 | 1 |
| BM (p) | 10 | 9 | 8 | 7 | 6 | 5 | 4 | 3 | 2 | 1 |

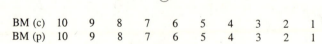

To Mary Kay, Alex, and Michael

Contents

Foreword

Businesses either grow or fade away. Growth can be achieved by consolidation, innovation, or diversification. The first option relies on economies of scale, synergies, and, hence, cost reduction to deliver better business performance. This is beneficial but eventually companies need to develop new markets and new products to thrive and grow. New products are the lifeblood of a successful business. Hence, many of the most important decisions a corporation makes are those concerning resource allocation to new product development and launch.

Forecasts are a crucial part of the information set needed to support these decisions. Assessing the impact and uptake of new technologies and the development of new markets is the high wire act of the forecaster's repertoire. Paradoxically, although the techniques required for new product forecasting are more sophisticated than those used for launched products, the resulting forecasts are subject to the highest levels of uncertainty and error. Furthermore, decisions based on these forecasts often irrevocably commit resources with little or no opportunity to adjust in the light of forecast inaccuracy. Therefore, organizations must not only create quality new product forecasts but also establish an effective decision-making process that does not ignore, but embraces the intrinsic uncertainty of new product forecasts. The present book authored by Dr. Kenneth Kahn aptly covers the essence of what new product forecasting really is within the applied context.

An overriding question is how one can obtain quality forecasts? As with all forecasts, the quality of the underlying assumptions is critical. Where the assumption is that the future will, by and large, mimic the past, simple extrapolation techniques may well suffice. However, in the case of new products, whether they are new to the corporation or new to the world, the past cannot be relied upon as a good predictor of the future and other techniques are needed. Crucially, there must be transparency in the way the underlying assumptions are quantified in the forecast model. Validation through objective challenge, the reduction of bias, gaining team consensus, and achieving management approval are impossible without such transparency. By concentrating on the key assumptions an organization will develop a collective understanding and record of the most important drivers of market share and also of the associated uncertainties. This has the additional benefit of limiting the tendency of senior managers to argue about the numbers in isolation. As Dr. Kahn correctly notes, new product forecasting can be conceived as a process of assumptions management.

In the course of assumptions management, it is important to differentiate between uncertainties that result in a "no go" decision, that is, zero sales, from those that influence the peak sales and uptake rate. Each assumption has an associated uncertainty and it is therefore necessary to quantify both the impact and likelihood of these within the forecast model. The methods available to do this are generally less developed than for forecasting per se and require a new set of skills from the new product forecaster. We applaud Dr. Kahn's effort to provide a reference on which to develop and hone one's new product forecasting skill set.

The reality is that many new product introductions fail but, in most cases, corporations are surprised and disappointed. New product forecasters have a crucial but frequently unpopular role in presenting unpalatable options to senior management. In general, it is the senior management teams that have to judge the risk they are prepared to take. Forecasts guide this judgment, communicating both the size of the opportunity, the possible outcomes, and the relative probability of these occurring. This reinforces Dr. Kahn's notion that new product forecasting should be viewed as a company process.

So far we have covered only the delivery of a quality forecast together with its associated levels of uncertainty. This forecast provides the touchstone of "the most likely outcome based on a single set of assumptions." It is only from this clear point of reference that the business can develop its plans.

The difference between forecasts and plans is fundamental. As defined in chapter 2, forecasts are indicative of what will likely happen, while plans are what management wants to happen. Consider what a Chief Financial Officer (CFO) needs either to communicate to the financial markets or to set a budget. Contrast the CFO's requirements with those of the Head of Manufacturing. The CFO's financial plans have to set expectations in the market and illustrate good corporate control; whereas the Head of Manufacturing has, in his manufacturing plan, to balance costs of capital and extra inventory against meeting top end sales expectations.

Now, given the inherent error in new product forecasts, which will be immediately clear when early sales are made, what do many businesses do? Do they compare the actual result with the original forecast and, if so, with what purpose? Do they compare it with a plan, for example, a budget number? Time now to remember that, by and large, the forecasts have been used to take irrevocable investment decisions on supporting development activities, building manufacturing capacity, or maybe ramping up sales capabilities. The virtuous circle can now be completed provided that the organization compares the actual outcome, not with a set of forecast numbers, but with the assumptions agreed at the beginning of the new product forecasting process. From this it can learn, refine methods, and adjust forecasts and plans, improving the basis for future decision making.

As Dr. Kahn stresses, a quality new product forecasting is more than simply a row of numbers. Hence, *New Product Forecasting: An Applied Approach* serves as a valuable new product forecasting reference. The reinforcing that there is a need to present and manage a clear set of assumptions and assess the uncertainty around these assumptions is paramount in our opinion. Doing so provides real business insight and a reflection of the overall brand strategy.

Martin Joseph
Head of Information Management & Forecasting

Alec Finney
Global Forecasting Manager
for the AstraZeneca Forecast Quality Network

Preface

Why Write This Book?

In the mid-1990s I was working with a technology company on a forecasting project. One of the activities during the project was developing a new product forecast for a second-generation digital camera. The forecasting team shared with me their frustration in trying to establish a forecast using diffusion modeling, even though they had thoroughly read literature on new product forecasting and inferred that diffusion models like the Bass model should be used, given overwhelming prevalence in the literature.

My response to the company was that diffusion models were not really appropriate for the task at hand, and that an easier, more explainable approach might be in order. Within about thirty minutes, I showed how a nonlinear regression model using an Excel spreadsheet could be developed and employed to provide a reasonable model for predicting the planned seven-month life cycle of the product. It was not sophisticated, and not overly accurate, but it was good enough to take to the management team for their feedback and adjustment. Marketing and sales ended up modifying the forecast based on functional expectations anyway. In short, the forecast that we developed in thirty minutes using a simple, applied approach served its purpose of being an initial baseline forecast on which to start discussions.

I soon conducted my own library research on new product forecasting and, surprisingly, found little information on the applied new product forecasting. Much work was statistical in nature, presenting new product forecasting as a statistical solution. This compelled me to propose to the Product Development and Management Association (PDMA) my conducting a study on new product forecasting practices, which was subsequently funded and conducted in 2000.

Since then I have presented to, worked with, and benchmarked a number of companies on the new product forecasting endeavor. What is clear is that many people without advanced knowledge in statistics are assigned the new product forecasting task. I thus believe that it is necessary to pose a simpler, less elusive view of new product forecasting. I also find that a balance of effort, time, and resources is needed as one develops new product forecasts; sometimes one can put in way too much effort, time, and resources and end up frustrated because management overrides the forecast. Keeping things simple should be the mantra. Finally, the statistical techniques published in the literature often require substantial data. In many cases, such data just does not exist or is too cost-prohibitive to obtain. All together, these issues exemplify that new product forecasting is more than a technique; it is a process that needs to be properly managed.

I certainly do not want to imply or overlook the value that statistics can bring to understanding the new product forecasting phenomenon. Rather, the standpoints of examples, figures, and narrative are necessary to provide a balanced view of how new product forecasting is often enacted within companies. Hence, I present the case for an applied approach to new product forecasting by way of this book.

Who Will Benefit from Reading This Book?

The objective of this book is to provide readers with a broad understanding of new product forecasting and the techniques that one can readily apply. Professionals should find this book a concise primer on new product forecasting and a welcome addition to the desk library as a reference for estimating new product demand. As well, this book should be a useful resource in advanced undergraduate, graduate, and executive education coursework, enlightening students to ways in which one can predict new product sales and market response. Such coursework would include demand forecasting, marketing analysis, marketing strategy, product development, and product management. Even engineering and technology management disciplines should find this book a good supplement to their product development and design coursework due to the need to critically understand new product sales and profitability for emerging technologies.

How Is This Book Organized?

Only eight chapters in total, this book provides a comprehensive, applied view of the new product forecasting endeavor. It is not meant to be an exhaustive discussion of new product forecasting, though. Instead, the intent is to introduce the topic and give enough information to instill confidence that new product forecasting can be managed and a meaningful forecast derived.

To accomplish this intent, the book is organized into three parts. Chapters 1 and 2 comprise Part I and address foundations of new product forecasting. Chapter 1 serves as the introduction to the topic of new product forecasting, and chapter 2 addresses process and structure issues related to new product forecasting and the broader process of new product development. Together these two chapters highlight the managerial side of new product forecasting and illuminate the practical issues that should be considered when developing new product forecasts, including the relationship between new product forecasting and the emerging process known as Sales and Operations Planning (S&OP).

Having established a new product forecasting foundation, an introduction to and discussion of new product forecasting techniques are in order in Part II. Chapter 3 introduces managerial judgment forecasting techniques, beginning with jury of executive opinion and ending with Markov process models. Chapter 4 introduces customer/market research techniques, beginning with concept tests and ending with conjoint analysis. Chapter 5 introduces the topic of times series data analysis on company data, moving from simple time series analysis methods to diffusion models. Chapter 6 introduces regression analysis, beginning with simple linear regression and going on to logistic regression. Earlier chapters address simpler forecasting techniques, while later chapters progress to more complicated techniques. Within each chapter the same flow occurs. Initial chapter discussions address basic, simpler forms of techniques found in that respective category of forecasting techniques; later chapter discussions progress to more advanced levels of techniques found in that respective category.

The last two chapters, 7 and 8, make up Part III and address special managerial considerations for new product forecasting. Chapter 7 discusses the launch phenomenon and continues through postlaunch. Important issues considered include cannibalization and supercession. Chapter 8 presents best practices and industry benchmarks for furthering one's understanding of and ability to improve new product forecasting efforts.

Acknowledgments

My appreciation goes out to the many colleagues both in academia and in industry who read through draft manuscripts and offered their constructive criticism. My appreciation also goes out to Harry Briggs and Elizabeth Granda, both of M.E. Sharpe, who guided me through the publication process. In addition, I am honored by the kind comments in the Foreword by Martin Joseph and Alec Finney, both of AstraZeneca, and the kind comments found on the cover of this book by Dr. Anthony Di Benedetto of Temple University and Mark Covas of the Gillette Company. Of course, no author can successfully complete a book project without support of family. My beloved appreciation to Mary Kay, Alex, and Michael for affording me their patience so that I could write this new product forecasting book.

Kenneth B. Kahn, Ph.D.

Part I

Foundations of Applied New Product Forecasting

The beginning of knowledge is the discovery
of something we do not understand.
Frank Herbert, Novelist (1920–1986)

It is important to first recognize and understand the distinguishing characteristics and challenges of new product forecasting before moving ahead and applying forecasting techniques. To meet these ends, chapter 1 introduces the topic of new product forecasting, describes the issues that make new product forecasting unique versus regular sales forecasting (especially the forecasting of existing products with a long, stable history), and defines key terminology associated with the new product forecasting topic. Chapter 1 also introduces the various techniques that one may consider to employ in the course of forecasting new products and links each technique to a particular new product forecasting strategy. Chapter 2 discusses and lays out the new product development process and the new product forecasting process. Chapter 2 further shows how these two processes are interrelated, and also how new product forecasting has an important, emerging role in the process known as Sales and Operations Planning (S&OP).

1

Introduction to Applied New Product Forecasting

New product forecasting is an important topic. Yet, compared to the forecasting of ongoing product demand and sales, new product forecasting receives considerably less attention, especially when counting the number of publications on each respective topic. Those publications that do discuss the topic of new product forecasting predominantly focus on statistically sophisticated techniques. This portrays new product forecasting as a potentially mysterious endeavor.

New product forecasting should not be viewed as mysterious. However, it certainly can be viewed as a complicated endeavor due to its many challenges. One principal challenge is overcoming the characteristically low credibility and low accuracy associated with new product forecasts. Benchmarking research finds that new product forecast accuracy on average one year after launch is slightly above 50 percent (Kahn 2002). Another major challenge is time management. When forecasting existing products, one can usually run a forecasting engine embedded within a company's production planning computer system, but, in contrast, forecasting a new product requires more manual attention, and thus, considerable time resources. The ability to afford additional time to develop a new product forecast may be prohibitive, particularly if a forecaster is responsible for a product mix of over ten thousand items. Less available time means less thinking on inherent new product forecasting issues like draw (the percent of a new product's volume coming from products within a product category), cannibalization (the percent of a new product's volume coming from other company products), category growth (the percent of a new product's volume coming from new category buyers who enter the category to purchase the new product), and category expansion (the percent of a new product's volume coming from increased category consumption among current category buyers where the purchase of the new product is incremental volume for the buyer). While high accuracy is never assured and time is a limited resource, employing a systematic approach can "demystify" the new product forecasting endeavor and force attention to those new products and issues deserving of attention. Subsequently, attending to the right issues initially can manifest more accurate new product forecasts and optimize one's time in generating this forecast. This therefore highlights taking a practical, applied approach to new product forecasting and acknowledging a process approach for proper new product forecasting.

To date, there is little guidance regarding applied new product forecasting and so it is the intent of this book to serve as a primer on new product forecasting with an applied approach perspective. Accordingly, this book outlines inherent issues in new product forecasting and discusses the application of different techniques for generating a new product forecast. A practical, "toolbox" approach is adopted to illustrate how various new product forecasts can be generated. In a toolbox approach, each new product forecasting technique is portrayed as a tool that has parameters regarding data input requirements, necessary statistical knowledge, and implicit assumptions; these characteristics then would indicate which forecasting technique to apply to the task at hand. Like someone attempting to use a screwdriver to pound a nail, some forecasting techniques are not well suited for certain forecasting situations because they can be overly time-consuming and result in erroneous ("broken") forecasts, especially if the forecaster fails to recognize the implicit assumptions on which the technique is based. To reiterate, one must have an understanding of the applied new product forecasting endeavor and which techniques are most appropriate in which situations before attempting to forecast new products. There is not one "save-all" or "silver bullet" technique for new product forecasting.

Clarifying the Terminology of Product, Service, or Offering

Before further discussions on the topic of new product forecasting, it is important to clarify what "product" means when conducting *new product forecasting*. This book adopts a broad definition for product, such that the term can describe any company offering, be it a product, service, or even an idea. The basis for this is that while historically and traditionally seen as distinct, products, services, and ideas are now innately intertwined. One does not just buy a new car: aside from receiving the car the buyer receives warranties, financing, and service opportunities. It therefore is very difficult, if not inappropriate, to distinguish products and services. There are slight nuances and inherent characteristics associated with products versus services versus ideas, yet the issues and processes related to the development and management of these are remarkably common and should be considered equivalent. Hence, the term "product" is used in conjunction with new product forecasting and employed throughout this book. The term "service" could be easily substituted, or simply the general terminology of "offering."

A New Product Forecasting Directive

A forecasting director during a recent executive training session commented, "I know the new product forecast is going to be wrong, but as long as the forecast can get us into the ballpark, we can plan accordingly." While this comment exemplifies the challenge that all new product forecasts are wrong, it further exemplifies a new product forecasting directive: to accept that error will exist and then work to develop the best, most meaningful forecast possible coupled with an understanding of what underlies the forecast and its associated contingencies. Doing so, the company can then plan financial, production, and other functional area decisions that pertain to the forthcoming new product. In short, the task of new product forecasting is laudable, and with understanding and persistence it can be accomplished.

Beginning the New Product Forecasting Endeavor

The first step toward successful new product forecasting is to establish the forecasting objective. This will clarify the purpose and intent of the forecast so that a meaningful forecast can be made—meaningful in the sense that the forecast is presented in a usable and understandable form. Otherwise, an innumerable set of forecasts can be developed, leading to confusion over which forecast should be employed. The forecasting objective helps to clarify what is needed at particular points during the new product development (NPD) process.

Once the forecasting objective is established, consideration is needed regarding the forecasting level, time horizon, interval, and form. Forecasting level refers the focal point in the corporate hierarchy where the new product forecast applies. Common levels include the stock keeping unit (SKU) level, stock keeping unit per location (SKUL) level, product line, strategic business unit (SBU) level, company level, and industry level. Forecasting time horizon refers to the time frame for how far out one should forecast. New product forecasts may correspond to a single point in the future or a series of forecasts extending out for a length of time (the latter is more common). Examples include a one- to two-year time horizon, which is typical for most fashion products, two to five years for most consumer product goods, and ten-plus years for pharmaceutical products. One reason for the longer time horizon for pharmaceuticals is the consideration paid to the length of term for a new drug patent. Forecasting time interval refers to the granularity of the new product forecast with respect to the time bucket as well as to how often the forecast might be updated. For example, a series of forecasts can be provided on a weekly, monthly, quarterly, or annual basis. Forecasting form refers to the unit of measure for the forecast. Typically, early new product forecasts are provided in monetary form (e.g., U.S. dollars) and later provided in terms of unit volume for production purposes. Some new product forecasts even come in the form of narrative scenarios that describe a future event.

Types of New Product Estimates

New product forecasts can represent different types of estimates. These include market potential, sales potential, market forecast, and sales forecast. Potential estimates represent the maximum attainable under a given set of conditions, with market pertaining to all companies within a given industry marketplace and sales pertaining to only the respective focal company. A market potential estimate is therefore a prediction of maximum total market volume under a given set of conditions. A sales potential estimate is a prediction of maximum company sales within the given market under a given set of conditions.

Forecasts represent likely or reasonable attainable estimates. A market forecast is therefore a reasonable estimate of total market volume to be attained by all firms in that market under a given set of conditions. A sales forecast is a reasonable estimate of attainable sales volume for a focal company within a given market under a given set of conditions.

These definitions characterize a market potential estimate as the largest, most general of the four types of estimates possible. A market forecast would be the next largest estimate. Sales potential would be the third largest estimate. The sales forecast would be the smallest and likely most granular of estimates. Note that in the case of a monopoly, market and sales estimates would be same; that is, in the case of a monopoly, market potential would equal sales potential, and the market forecast would equal the sales forecast.

New Product Planning Versus New Product Forecasting

New product planning and new product forecasting should be keenly distinguished, although in many companies this distinction is muddled. New product planning is a process that determines company management expectation of what sales volume or revenue should be to meet company financial objectives and financial targets. In other words, new product planning is keenly focused on what management wants to happen at new product launch and postlaunch. New product forecasting is a process that determines a reasonable estimate of sales attainable under a given set of conditions. That is, new product forecasting serves as a reality check by providing visibility to what is likely to happen.

Many times during the new product forecasting endeavor company management expectations are driven by financial objectives and financial targets, which influences the new product forecast, often in the direction of an inflated one. All efforts should be made to resist these temptations to tweak forecasts unless a set of reasonable assumptions and conditions can be provided to support a different forecast. Objectivity is vital when deriving a new product forecast.

Types of New Products

A misnomer for new product forecasting is the general presumption that all new products correspond to major changes and major new product initiatives. By definition, there are seven different types of new products, including cost reductions, product improvements, line extensions, new markets, new uses, new category entries, and new-to-the-world products.

Cost reductions are not dramatic changes to the product, but those that can influence consumer purchase behavior, especially when connected with implementing a new pricing policy or sustaining a cost advantage. Wyndham's 2004 announcement to reduce minibar prices across its hotels is indicative of a cost reduction (Wyndham.com). Product improvements are product enhancements that improve the product's form or function and are often labeled as "new and improved" or "better flavor." General Mills' promotion of larger marshmallows in its Lucky Charms cereal is indicative of a product improvement (General Mills.com). Line extensions retain standard features of an original product (or set of products) and add unique features that the original product (or original set of products) does not have. The distinction between a product improvement and line extension is that the product improvement replaces (supercedes) the original product, so customers are migrated to the new product, while in the case of a line extension both the original and new products are available for purchase. Kellogg's introduction of chocolate chip cookie flavored Eggo waffles represents a line extension (Kelloggs.com).

New uses are original products positioned in new markets without changing, or only slightly changing, the original product. The classic example of this type of new use product is Arm & Hammer baking soda, which was originally positioned as a baking product, but later as a deodorizer to open up a huge market. New market products are when a company takes its product to a new market where the product had not been offered. For example, Gillette, having previously launched the Venus Divine women's shaver in the United States and Canada, announced the launch of the Venus Divine shaver to Australia in late 2004 (*Food Week Magazine* 2004). New category entries are products that are new to the company, but as a category, not new to the consumer. McDonald's foray into clothing with McKids clothing is an example of a new category entry (BBC News). New-to-the-world products are technological innovations that create a completely new market that previously did not exist. These innovations would be characterized as discontinuous innovations, where the new product introduces a product technology previously not available to the marketplace. Launching the first AIDS vaccine would be indicative of a new-to-the-world product.

These seven products can be organized along four dimensions characterized by the type of market to be served (current or new customers) and type of product technology (current or new technology). Current customers represent customers currently associated with the target market or market segment who may be an immediate customer, a competi-

Figure 1.1 **The Product-Market Matrix**

Product Technology

	Current	New
Current	**Market Penetration** (Cost Reductions, Product Improvements)	**Product Development** (Line Extensions)
New	**Market Development** (New Uses, New Markets)	**Diversification** (New-to-the-Company, New-to-the-World)

Market (row axis label, spanning Current/New)

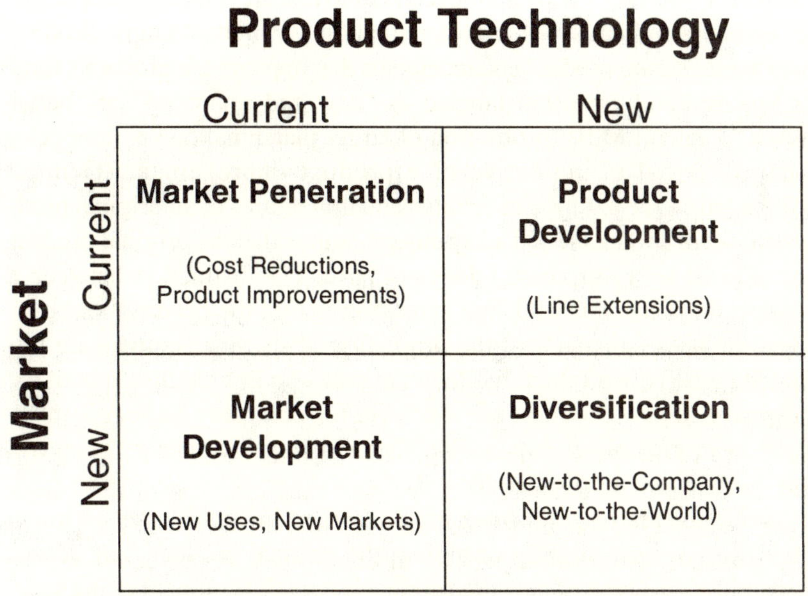

tor customer, or a noncustomer (a potential customer that has not made a purchase yet). Current product technology means the company has the technology, while new technology indicates that the respective technology is novel. The framework shown in Figure 1.1 illustrates a framework called the product-market matrix.

As portrayed in Figure 1.1, the current market (current customers) being served by a new product using current product technology is indicative of a market penetration strategy. A market penetration strategy has the objective to increase market share or increase product usage. The current customer base is pursued with no major changes to the existing product technology. Cost reductions and product improvements are characteristic of a market penetration strategy because these two types of new products attempt to attract customers through a new pricing policy or improved features.

A product development strategy derives from an objective to capitalize on existing product technology and offer more options to the customer base. In this way, the company with a more diverse product line can fend off competitors. Line extensions are characteristically associated with a product development strategy.

A market development strategy stems from a desire to expand sales volume of existing products through new markets. This would include geographic expansions, including international markets and targeting new market segments within the domestic market. A market development strategy relies on the current predominant product technology and tries to find viable new markets that will respond favorably to such technology. New uses and new market products are characteristic of a market development strategy.

Diversification is pursued when the company wishes to expand its business into related businesses and unrelated businesses. A company pursuing this strategy confronts complexities associated with new customer markets and new product technologies. New category entries and new-to-the-world products are pursued in the course of a diversification strategy.

Figure 1.1 illustrates that new product planning becomes more complex and riskier as companies move down the diagonal of the matrix from the upper left quadrant (market penetration) to the lower right quadrant (diversification). Plotting the different types of new products, the riskier projects are those associated with new category entries and new-to-the-world products. This is because the market and product technology are unfamiliar and untested from the perspective of the company. The least risky products are those associated with cost reductions and product improvements. This is because company data, information, and knowledge of the market and product technology are preexisting, thereby offering a more comfortable business situation for the company. Because most, if not all, companies launch more than one new product annually, typically launching a portfolio of new products that include products from all four cells, a number of new product forecasts will pervade the company at any given time. This reinforces the need for a systematic, process approach to new product forecasting.

New Product Forecasting Techniques

While new product forecasting should be managed as a process, new product forecasting techniques are a critical component of this process in establishing a meaningful starting point on which to begin the process. Consequently, the majority of this book discusses the different ways in which a meaningful starting point can be generated.

Generally there are five categories of new product forecasting techniques. These include judgmental techniques, customer/market research techniques, time series analyses, regression analyses, and other quantitative techniques. Figure 1.2 presents these five categories along with the more popular techniques that fall into each of the five categories.

Judgment techniques represent those techniques that attempt to turn experience, judgments, and intuition into formal forecasts. Six popular techniques within this category include:

- Jury of executive opinion: a top-down forecasting technique where the forecast is arrived at through the ad hoc combination of opinions and predictions made by informed executives and experts.
- Sales force composite: a bottoms-up forecasting technique where individuals (typically salespeople) provide their forecasts. These forecasts are then aggregated to calculate a higher-level forecast.
- Scenario analysis: an analysis involving the development of scenarios to predict the future. Two types of scenario analysis include exploratory and normative approaches. Exploratory scenario analysis starts in the present and moves out to the future based on current trends. Normative scenario analysis leaps out to the future and works back to determine what should be done to achieve what is expected to occur.
- Delphi method: a technique based on subjective expert opinion gathered through several structured anonymous rounds of data collection. Each successive round provides consolidated feedback to the respondents, and the forecast is further refined. The objective of the Delphi method is to capture the advantages of multiple experts in a committee, while minimizing the effects of social pressure to agree with the majority, ego pressure to stick with your original forecast despite new information, the influence of a repetitive argument, and the influence of a dominant individual.
- Decision trees: a probabilistic approach to forecasting where various contingencies and their associated probability of occurring are determined—typically in a subjective fashion.
- Assumptions-based modeling: a technique that attempts to model the behavior of the relevant market environment by breaking the market down into market drivers. Then by assuming values for these drivers, forecasts are generated. These models are also referred to as chain models or market breakdown models.

Figure 1.2 **Sample of New Product Forecasting Techniques**

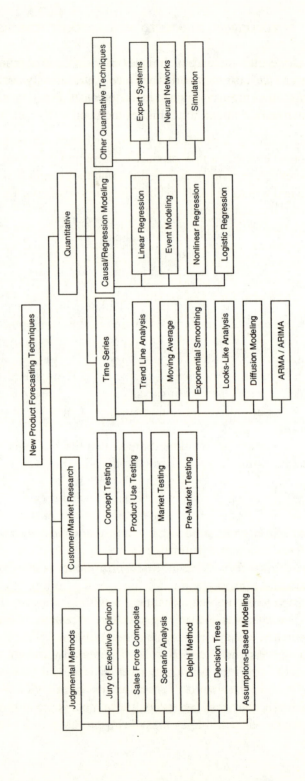

Customer/market research techniques include those approaches that collect data on the customer/market and then systematically analyze these data to draw inferences on which to make forecasts. Four general classes of customer/market research techniques include:

- Concept testing: a process by which customers (current or potential ones) evaluate a new product concept and give their opinions on whether the concept is something that they might have an interest in and would be likely to buy. The purpose of concept testing is to proof the new product concept.
- Product use testing: a process by which customers (current or potential ones) evaluate a product's functional characteristics and performance. The purpose of product use testing is to proof the product's functionality.
- Market testing: a process by which targeted customers evaluate the marketing plan for a new product in a market setting. The purpose of market testing is to proof the proposed marketing plan and the "final" new product.
- Premarket testing: a procedure that uses syndicated data and primary consumer research to estimate the sales potential of new product initiatives. Assessor and BASES are two proprietary new product forecasting models associated with premarket testing. BASES is commonly employed in the consumer products goods industry.

Time series techniques analyze sales data to detect historical "sales" patterns and construct a representative graph or formula to project sales into the future. Time series techniques used in association with new product forecasting include:

- Trend line analysis: a line is fit to a set of data. This is done either graphically or mathematically.
- Moving average: a technique that averages only a specified number of previous sales periods.
- Exponential smoothing techniques: a set of techniques that develops forecasts by addressing the forecast components of level, trend, seasonality, and cycle. Weights or smoothing coefficients for each of these components are determined statistically and are applied to "smooth" previous period information (see Makridakis, Wheelwright, and Hyndman 1997; Mentzer and Bienstock 1998).
- Looks-like analysis (analogous forecasting): a technique that attempts to map sales of other products onto the product being fore-

cast. Looks-like analysis is a popular technique applied to line extensions by using sales of previous product line introductions to profile sales of the new product.

- Diffusion models: models that estimate the growth rate of product sales by considering various factors influencing the consumer adoption process. Considerations taken into account include the rate at which mass media (the coefficient of innovation) and word of mouth (the coefficient of imitation) affect lead user, early adopter, early majority, late majority, and laggard customer segments. Different types of diffusion models exist including the Bass Model, Gompertz curve, and logistic curve. Diffusion models are also referred to as technology S-curves (see Morrison 1996; Mahajan, Muller, and Wind 2000).

- Autoregressive moving average (ARMA) / autoregressive integrated moving average (ARIMA) models: a set of advanced statistical approaches to forecasting that incorporate key elements of both time series and regression model building. Three basic activities (or stages) are considered: (1) identifying the model, (2) determining the model's parameters, and (3) testing/applying the model. Critical in using any of these techniques is understanding the concepts of autocorrelation and differencing. ARMA/ARIMA models are also referred to as Box-Jenkins techniques (see Makridakis et al. 1997).

Regression analysis techniques use exogenous or independent variables and, through statistical methods, develop formula correlating these with a dependent variable. While sometimes referred to as "causal" models, these models are predicated on correlational relationships and do not reflect true cause and effect relationships. Four popular techniques within this subcategory include:

- Linear regression: a statistical methodology that assesses the relation between one or more managerial variables and a dependent variable (sales), strictly assuming that these relationships are linear in nature. For example, price may be an important driver of new product sales. The relationship between price and the quantity sold would be determined from prior data of other products within the product line and then used to predict sales for the forthcoming product.
- Event modeling: often a linear regression-based methodology that assesses the relation between one or more events, whether company-

initiated or nonaffiliated with the company, and a dependent variable (sales). For example, a promotion used with prior product launches would be analyzed and the bump in sales caused by this promotion statistically determined. The expected bump in sales would be correspondingly mapped to the sales of the new product.

- Nonlinear regression: a statistical methodology that assesses the relation between one or more managerial variables and a dependent variable (sales), but these relationships are not necessarily assumed to be linear in nature.
- Logistic regression: a statistical methodology that assesses the relation between one or more managerial variables and a binary outcome, such as purchase versus nonpurchase. A logistic regression model calculates the probability of an event occurring or not occurring.

The other quantitative techniques category includes those techniques that employ unique methodologies or represent a hybrid of time series and regression techniques. A sample of these forecasting techniques include the following:

- Expert systems: typically computer-based heuristics or rules for forecasting. These rules are determined by interviewing forecasting experts and then constructing "if-then" statements. Forecasts are generated by going through various applicable if-then statements until all statements have been considered.
- Neural networks: advanced statistical models that attempt to decipher patterns in a particular sales time series. These models can be time-consuming to build and difficult to explain. In most cases, these models are proprietary.
- Simulation: an approach to incorporate market forces into a decision model. "What-if" scenarios are then considered. Normally, simulation is computer-based. A typical simulation model is Monte Carlo simulation, which employs randomly generated events to drive the model and assess outcomes.

New Product Forecasting Strategy: Linking Techniques to Type of New Product

Because of the available data and nuances of the marketplace, each type of new product reflects different scenarios and needs for new product

Figure 1.3 **New Product Forecasting Strategies**

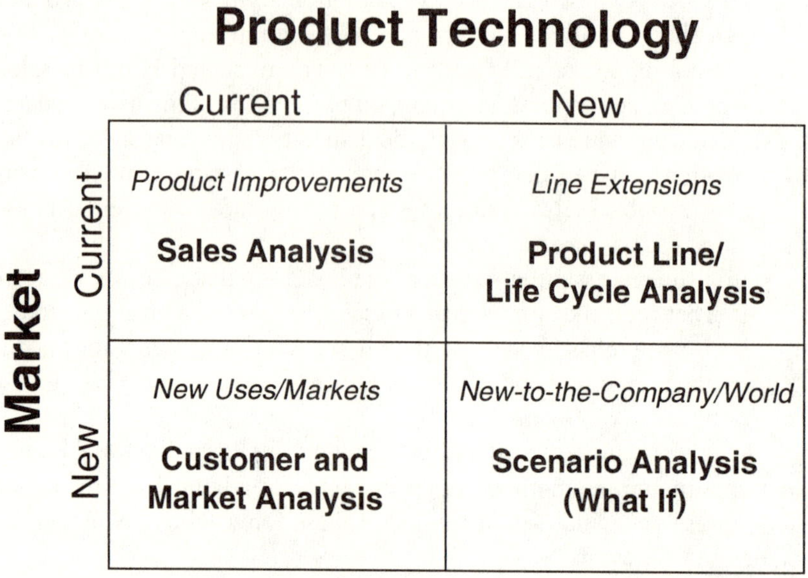

Product Technology

		Current	New
Market	**Current**	*Product Improvements* **Sales Analysis**	*Line Extensions* **Product Line/ Life Cycle Analysis**
	New	*New Uses/Markets* **Customer and Market Analysis**	*New-to-the-Company/World* **Scenario Analysis (What If)**

forecasting. And while there are a number of forecasting techniques available, it is important to realize that not all of them are appropriate for every forecasting situation. Judgmental techniques are quite adaptable, but very time-consuming; they would therefore not be appropriate in situations where a severe time constraint exists. Quantitative techniques like time series and regression analyses require data, and rely on the critical assumption that current data will correspond to future states; if the data are not available and the assumption of market stability not feasible, quantitative techniques would not be meaningful. Customer/market research techniques are time-consuming and expensive to perform, although beneficial to understanding market forces and customer preferences. Budget constraints could seriously hamper what degree of customer/market research may be undertaken. Accounting for all these considerations reinforces one's adoption of a toolbox approach for applying new product forecasting techniques.

To assist in decisions related to new product forecasting, a variation of the product-market matrix is offered to reveal four new product forecasting situations (refer to Figure 1.3). Mapping market uncertainty and product technology uncertainty on the two dimensions of current and new reveals four cells, each of which is represented by one of the following new product forecasting strategies: sales analysis, life-cycle analysis, customer and market analysis, and scenario analysis.

A new product forecasting strategy of sales analysis is associated with the situation of current market and current product technology, where the uncertainties of market and product technology are lowest. Cost reductions and product improvements would populate this cell. The nature of these products would signify that sales data are available because the product has previously existed. Analysis would focus on looking for deviations and deflections in sales patterns based on previous cost reductions and improvements in the product. Quantitative techniques such as times series and regression could be quite useful in achieving objective forecasts.

A product life cycle analysis strategy is associated with the situation of current market and new technology. Line extensions are associated with this cell and represent higher product technology uncertainty. Because of understanding with the current marketplace, analyses would attempt to overlay patterns of previously launched products in the product line onto the new line extensions. These patterns would characterize a launch curve or life cycle curve by way of looks-like analysis or analogous forecasting.

A customer/market analysis strategy would be necessary in the case of current technology and a new market due to higher market uncertainty. The purpose of this forecasting strategy is to understand the new market and therefore reduce such uncertainty and manifest greater understanding about the new market. Various customer/market research studies might be engaged along with the use of assumptions-based models in an attempt to specify market drivers, which would be validated by the customer/market research performed. Products in this cell include new use and new market products (market extensions).

A scenario analysis strategy corresponds to the situation of new market and new product technology, representing high market and product technology uncertainties akin to new-to-the-company (new category entries) and new-to-the-world products. Scenario analysis would be employed to paint a picture of the future and future directions to be taken. Note that a scenario analysis strategy should not be confused with simply the use of scenario analysis; rather the intent of forecasting in this situation is to develop various scenarios on which to base the NPD decision. Given a lack of data, the potential difficulty in identifying the specific target market, and questions regarding technology acceptance, judgmental assessment techniques would play a major role in this cell.

It should be recognized that forecasting techniques have applicability across all of the cells. However, depending on the specific situation, some techniques are better suited for the task at hand. The resources necessary and outcome desired also will dictate which techniques are better suited for the task at hand. For example, customer/market research could greatly benefit market understanding related to cost reductions, product improvements, and line extensions. These techniques can be resource-consuming in terms of cost, personnel, and time, however. Managerial judgment techniques can be readily applied to all types of new products. Yet, often these techniques will not provide enough lower-level detail, as in the case of a product improvement for instance. Hence, the intent of the proposed framework is to offer a strategy to facilitate the new product forecasting effort by suggesting the application of those techniques that appear to be most appropriate.

Key Concepts

New Product Forecasting Directive
Clarifying Product, Service, or Offering
New Product Planning versus New Product Forecasting
Types of New Products
Types of New Product Forecasting Techniques
New Product Forecasting Strategy

Discussion Questions

1. What might be the objective(s) of new product forecasting?
2. What differences do products and services have with regard to new product forecasting?
3. What is the difference between new product planning and new product forecasting?
4. What are the four general marketing strategies related to new products? Which new product types fall into each of these four general strategies?
5. What are the four general categories of new product forecasting techniques?
6. How might type of new product affect the new product forecasting effort?

2

New Product Development and New Product Forecasting: Process and Structure

While literary attention has emphasized techniques, new product forecasting is more than establishing a numeric forecast. New product forecasting should serve to enlighten and offer greater understanding around the new business, identification of key assumptions, likely business drivers, coordination of business capabilities, better resource distribution, and improved visibility to and management of inventory and customer service levels—all depending on the forecasting objective. A numeric forecast, by itself, does not provide such enlightenment and understanding, nor is a numeric forecast alone a cure-all for achieving new product success. New product forecasts must be commonly understood and successfully link the functional entities in the company like finance, marketing, manufacturing/operations, procurement, R&D, and sales. Such linkage is manifested by *meaningful* forecasts: forecasts that can be readily translated and employed by the multiple functions involved.

Meaningful forecasts highlight the need to consider new product forecasting from a process perspective. Recognition of new product forecasting as a *process* exemplifies the need to recognize new product forecasting as truly a corporate-wide endeavor that traverses company politics and functional domains to provide a basis on which to predicate new product business decisions. Process mandates that this company endeavor derive a *meaningful* estimate of attainable demand under a given set of conditions. New product forecasting should therefore not be viewed as just a numeric output from a computer system, a computer software package, or a statistical technique. Numbers, data, formula, and computer capability are subsumed within the broader context of the new product forecasting process. The process of new product forecasting is subsumed within the broader context of the new product development process.

The New Product Development Process

New product forecasting is a critical part of the overriding new product development (NPD) process. Thus, it is necessary to understanding the nature and interplay of issues between NPD and new product forecasting.

The NPD process encompasses a series of stages and gates, and is normally referred to as a Stage-Gate™ process (see Figure 2.1). Each stage represents a distinct set of related activities, normally grouped into the following five stages: (1) strategic planning, (2) concept generation, (3) pretechnical evaluation, (4) technical development, and (5) commercialization. Product launch, also termed new product introduction (NPI), occurs at the end of the commercialization stage. Following launch, the separate process of product life-cycle management (PLCM) begins.

Preestablished gate criteria serve as screening material and must be satisfied before a "product" can enter subsequent NPD process stages. Gate criteria in the strategic planning stage will address issues of market size and technical feasibility to proof a market opportunity ("product" here is a statement of market opportunity). Gate criteria in the concept generation and pretechnical evaluation stages will need details of market interest in a product concept, market viability, revenue potential, and ability to technically delivery the new product technology ("product" here is a product concept statement). During technical development the product becomes realized, meaning that a tangible prototype is created and evaluated on both market and technical feasibility dimensions ("product" here is a prototype). Commercialization is when the product takes its ultimate form, and marketing plans are evaluated. Hard data is needed to support key launch decisions, and thus, all testing initiatives during the commercialization would serve to qualify key forecasting assumptions and solidify sales forecasts.

Because each gate pertains to different types of decisions corresponding to different stages of activities within the new product development process, new product forecasts will differ across NPD stages. For example, forecasting during the strategic planning stage will often focus on market potential and sales potential estimates. These forecasts would be financial in nature to answer the question of whether the market opportunity represented a valid pursuit. Marketing and finance departments would play key roles in generating these forecasts.

During concept generation and pretechnical evaluation stages, fore-

Figure 2.1 **The New Product Development Process**

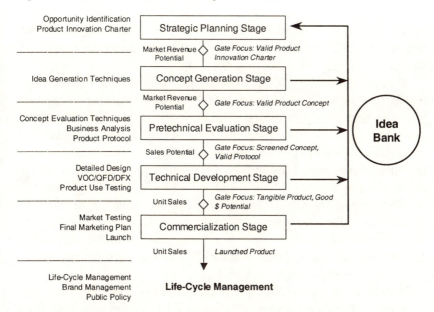

casts focus predominantly on sales potential estimates to answer the question of whether the product concept is a worthwhile idea for the company to pursue. Forecasts would normally take a financial form under the auspices of marketing and finance departments.

Forecasts in the technical development stage transition from sales potential estimates to unit volume sales forecasts. Forecasts during the technical development stage are used to organize production operations, including purchasing and installing possible new equipment and dies, procuring raw materials, and scheduling human resource requirements. Marketing and manufacturing oversee the forecasting endeavor at this point.

During the commercialization phase, unit sales forecasts are critical. These forecasts take financial form to validate marketing budgets and unit volume form for purposes of operations and supply management. Marketing, manufacturing, and supply chain are key players in the development of the new product forecast in this stage.

Using Teams to Structure New Product Development

All companies will employ some form of team to manage NPD activities. Teams represent a temporary organization structure focusing on

the achievement of a specific objective. While the organization structure biases the types of teams that a particular company might use, there
are generally five types of teams: functional, multifunctional, balanced
matrix, project matrix, and venture teams. The characteristics of each of
these types of teams are shown in Table 2.1.

A functional team works within an individual department with mini-
mal to no contact with other department personnel. Activities best served
by a functional team would be department-specific activities that are
narrow in scope and have a specific, distinct goal, for example, electri-
cal engineering personnel working on a solution to a power "glitch" in a
new amplifier system. The addition of other department personnel would
not necessarily benefit the project and, in fact, could inhibit engineering's
ability to resolve the matter in a cost-effective and timely fashion. Functional teams have a team leader from the given department, and are under the auspices of the respective department and that respective
department's manager. Rewards and recognition are 100 percent the responsibility of the department manager.

Multifunctional teams are a predominant form of team and employed
for both product development and product management purposes. Multifunctional teams comprise personnel from those departments having
skills necessary to achieve the team's objectives. In some respects, multifunctional team members are liaisons to the team, representing each of
their respective department's views. The team leader may be one of these
team representatives or a preselected team leader outside of the departments, for example, a product development, product management, or
project management department. This team leader directs the project
effort, but has no control of rewards and recognitions since such compensation is still 100 percent from each representative's department. This
is a disadvantage because loyalty to the team initiative may be low, leading to lower motivation to work on the project. Multifunctional teams
also contend with interdepartmental conflict because each team member represents their own departments' views. Nonetheless, multifunctional teams offer an ability to be flexible for many situations.

Balanced matrix teams also are composed of representatives from
different departments, with a preselected team leader from a department responsible for team management, for example, product development, product management, or project management. The distinction of
balanced matrix teams is that team member rewards and recognitions
are split equally between the respective team member's department and

Table 2.1

New Product Development Teams

	Functional team	Multifunctional team	Balanced matrix	Cross-functional team	Venture team
Department representation	Single department	Multiple departments	Multiple departments	Multiple departments	Multiple departments
Accountable to	100% department	Mostly department	50% department, 50% team	Mostly team	100% team
Appropriate product development projects	Cost improvements, simple product improvements	All types of product development projects	All types of product development projects	All types of product development projects	New category entries, new-to-the-world products
Issues	Focuses on single, specific product issue	Addresses issue affecting multiple departments, but conflict can arise due to team members' loyalties to their own department	Team member confusion can arise due to uncertainty over equally splitting time between department and team	Team members work on team issues predominantly, although there are departmental responsibilities as well	Personnel removed from organization to address key corporate objective(s); department managers may resist this

the team. That is, 50 percent of an employee's rewards and recognition is decided by the department, and 50 percent is decided by the team leader. The advantage of balanced matrix teams is an attempt to equalize the team effort with department efforts. Unfortunately, it becomes very difficult to equalize team and department efforts, leading to team member confusion over compensation and conflicts between department managers and team leaders over team member responsibilities. Balanced matrix teams are not very common due to the complexity surrounding rewards and recognition to team members.

Cross-functional teams, also called project matrix teams, are composed of representatives from different departments with a preselected team leader from a department responsible for team management. The distinction of cross-functional teams is that team member rewards and recognition are mostly the responsibility of the team leader. This means that team members are mostly dedicated to the project. While there still can be conflict between department and team priorities and responsibilities, cross-functional teams provide a greater focus on the part of team members.

Venture teams are when team members are pulled out of their departments to serve on a self-contained team and these team members' time is 100 percent dedicated to the project. There can be resistance to venture teams by department managers because there is the possibility that the best people will be pulled out of their departments to serve on the venture team. There also is the need to provide adequate resources to support a stand-alone team. However, venture teams offer the advantage of being completely focused on the given task. Because of these issues, venture teams are typically reserved for new-to-the-world product development projects. This leads to another, more subtle, reason for the use of venture teams in that there is the possibility of creating a new division around the venture team should the resulting product be successful. Even more subtly, the separating of the venture team allows the opportunity for the company to more easily sell off the new division (venture team) should company management decide that the developed product is outside of corporate objectives.

Two types of venture teams are possible. An in-house venture team is one that meets with the company infrastructure and facilities. A spinout venture team is when the team meets at a different location and creates its own quasi-organization, if not an entirely new organization. The latter type of venture team obviously is more expensive to support, given the duplication of resources.

Distinguishing the Core Team, the Ad-Hoc Team, and the Extended Team

For each of the above types of teams, there is an implicit team structure. This structure encompasses a core team, an ad-hoc team, and an extended team. The core team is the original, permanent team members who represent the key skill sets necessary for achieving the team's given objective. The ad-hoc team represents team members who are added when specialized skills or knowledge outside of the team skill/ knowledge set are needed. For example, purchasing may be added to a product development team if discussions of how to acquire a new material persist. Ad-hoc team members remain on the team only for as long as they are needed. The extended team represents support personnel that help the core team to accomplish its given objective. Administrative staff are characteristically members of the extended team.

Development and Launch Teams

During the commercialization stage, the development team transfers responsibility for the new product to the launch team. The launch team takes the reins of the new product, presenting the final forecast and launch schedule during the Sales and Operations Planning (S&OP) process, which will be discussed later in this chapter. Hence, the launch team plays a particularly key role in new product forecasting.

Unfortunately, the hand-off between the development team and the launch team, albeit critical, is often mishandled. An over-the-wall approach is typical, meaning that new people assume responsibilities for the product without much direction or cross-communication between the two teams. New product forecasting, especially its assumptions and their rationales, is not communicated clearly, if at all. This emphasizes the need for a separate process to ensure better management of the hand-off between the development team and the launch team. And the fact that a separate new product forecast input is needed as a recognized part of S&OP further implies a need for a distinct new product forecasting process.

The New Product Forecasting Process

While regular sales forecasting is a distinctly recognized process, a number of companies are now realizing that new product forecasting is deserving of a separate process as well. This is because new product forecasting has different inputs compared to the regular sales forecasting process. Doing so highlights the importance of new product forecasting and draws attention to the endeavor. Otherwise, new product forecasting gets intertwined with regular forecasting and often is overlooked by ongoing business initiatives. If separated out, new product tracking also becomes a priority.

Like regular sales forecasting, new product forecasting comprises distinct steps. But unlike regular sales forecasting, these steps vary as the new product takes more definitive form, moving from early to later NPD process stages. However, the number of new product forecasting steps increases and they become more complex as the problem approaches the launch point. This is because forecasts related to the launch are more critical for business decisions as the launch approaches, and thus, more attention to detail is required. This highlights the interplay between NPD and new product forecasting. Figure 2.2 illustrates the likely process issues, steps, and decisions per NPD stage.

Strategic Planning

The objective of the strategic planning stage is to qualify market opportunity. Forecasts at this early stage take a financial form pertaining to market and sales potential estimates. These estimates represent initial baseline forecasts on which to predicate the decision to go/no-go with the new product opportunity. Before deriving these estimates, careful identification, qualification, and quantification of forecasting assumptions are necessary. New product forecasting comprises the following two steps during strategic planning:

SP1. *Establish New Product Forecast Assumptions:* Identify, qualify, and quantify key assumptions to help scope and derive market opportunity potential estimates.

SP2. *Generate Baseline Market Potential Forecast:* Use the established assumptions and present an initial base case estimate, if not a range of case estimates, for market and sales potential for the new product opportunity.

Concept Generation

Sales potential becomes the focus during the concept generation phase to determine concepts that are more market worthy. Much of the activity

Figure 2.2 **Steps of the New Product Forecasting Process**

New Product Forecasting Process

Strategic Planning
Establish new product forecast assumptions
Generate baseline market potential forecast

Concept Generation
Review and verify new product forecast assumptions
Revise new product forecast assumptions
Generate baseline sales revenue potential forecast

Pretechnical Evaluation
Review and verify new product forecast assumptions
Revise new product forecast assumptions
Generate baseline sales revenue potential forecast
Issue baseline sales forecast
Establish a calendar for the new product
Approve the product protocol prior to technical development resources commitment

Technical Development
Review and verify new product forecast assumptions
Revise new product forecast assumptions
Review and verify the NPD calendar
Generate baseline unit sales forecast
Adjust baseline unit sales forecast
Approve baseline unit sales forecast

Commercialization
Review and verify new product forecast assumptions
Revise new product forecast assumptions
Generate baseline unit sales forecast
Adjust baseline unit sales forecast
Apply supply chain constraints
Approve unit sales forecast as part of S&OP process
Construct launch control protocol

Postlaunch
New product forecasting transitions to regular sales forecasting after first six periods of
   sales activity (usually after the first six months)
New product forecast accuracy tracked during the first year and reported during the
   S&OP reporting process
Track critical issues labeled in the launch control protocol
Enact launch control protocol if trigger points are reached

during this phase will be constructing and testing concept statements, and using results to put together sales potential estimates. Results also should be used to verify, and revise if needed, assumptions made during the strategic planning stage. New product forecasting comprises the following three steps during concept generation:

> *CG1. Review and Verify New Product Forecast Assumptions:* Recall and appraise assumptions made in the strategic planning stage. Determine which assumptions remain valid, and which are incorrect or too vague.

CG2. *Revise New Product Forecast Assumptions:* Update assumptions as deemed necessary. Add new assumptions considered important to determining new product sales potential.

CG3. *Generate Baseline Sales Revenue Potential Forecast:* Recalculate sales potential based on the updated assumptions and possible new assumptions.

Pretechnical Evaluation

Pretechnical evaluation further hones the sales potential forecast on which concepts deserve to be developed and culminates with a preliminary sales forecast. More testing is conducted to validate and verify new product forecasting assumptions, and introduce new assumptions if needed. Forecasts at the end of this stage are critical because it is these forecasts that underlie decisions to move forward into technical development and incur substantial resource commitment. These forecasts are in financial form to gauge new product profitability and in unit volume form to gauge the size of manufacturing resource requirements. Because substantial resource commitments hinge on these forecasts, an approval step is prescribed to ensure that forecasts are reviewed across the company and receive management attention. Four new product forecasting steps in the pretechnical evaluation stage are presented:

PTE1. *Review and Verify New Product Forecast Assumptions:* Recall and reappraise assumptions from the strategic planning and concept generation stages. Determine which assumptions remain valid, and which are incorrect or too vague.

PTE2. *Revise New Product Forecast Assumptions:* Update all assumptions as deemed necessary. Add new assumptions considered important to determining new product sales potential.

PTE3. *Reissue Baseline Sales Revenue Potential Forecast:* Recalculate sales potential based on the updated assumptions and possible new assumptions.

PTE4. *Issue Baseline Sales Forecast:* Take the sales potential information along with modified and new assumptions and calculate a preliminary sales forecast. This will likely involve several meetings to solidify a sales forecast that will then be presented to management for approval. The baseline sales forecast is included in the product protocol document (refer to Crawford and Di Benedetto 2000, 2003 for more information on product protocols; also refer to chapter 7).

PTE5. *Establish a Calendar for the New Product:* Given assumptions and forecast data, marketing/product management and development/engineering meet to set an NPD calendar and propose a forthcoming launch date. This calendar outlining the schedule of forthcoming activities is included in the product protocol document.

PTE6. *Approve the Product Protocol Prior to Technical Development Resources Commitment:* A management review meeting is held to approve the product protocol, which includes critical information such as the sales forecast, NPD calendar, and proposed product specifications. The management review team must decide whether further resources will be committed to develop and realize the product concept.

Technical Development

During technical development, greater attention is given to unit volume sales forecasts to help manufacturing/operations secure appropriate capacity, tooling, and other resources. Financial forecasts are prevalent too, though, to assist in establishing preliminary company financial targets, marketing budgets, and sales quotas. More testing in this stage will focus on product technology functionality, although assumptions related to customer response can be evaluated in the course of testing. As all functions more intently consider the new product due to the resource commitment, discussions on the new product begin to emerge during the company's S&OP process. The general steps of set baseline forecast, adjust forecast, and approve forecast now become ingrained in the new product forecasting process. The following five new product forecasting steps are envisioned during technical development:

TD1. *Review and Verify New Product Forecast Assumptions:* Recall and reappraise assumptions established in previous NPD stages. Determine which assumptions remain valid, and which are incorrect or too vague.

TD2. *Revise New Product Forecast Assumptions:* Update all assumptions as deemed necessary. Add new assumptions considered important to determining new product sales forecasts, both from financial and unit volume perspectives.

TD3. *Review and Verify the NPD Calendar:* Given the updated assumptions and new assumptions pertaining to such issues as changing market dynamics, technology issues, and so on, the NPD team determines whether the new product is on schedule or whether the NPD calendar should be modified to reflect a new timetable.

TD4. *Generate Baseline Unit Sales Forecast:* Incorporate available data based on to-date assumptions and calculate financial and unit volume sales forecasts.

TD5. *Adjust Baseline Unit Sales Forecast:* Issue forecasts out to marketing/product management, sales, manufacturing/operations, and finance for appraisal. Allow each functional area to provide feedback on the issued forecasts. Through several meetings, feedback is reconciled into establishing financial and unit volume sales forecasts.

TD6. *Approve Baseline Unit Sales Forecast:* A management review meeting approves the sales forecasts and the updated NPD calendar. This sets the stage for the new product's eventual launch.

Commercialization

The commercialization stage culminates with the launch of the new product. Forecasts are critical to finalizing financial targets, marketing budgets, and sales quotas. Particular attention keenly focuses on unit sales volume to support account shipments and meet expected consumer demand through decisions related to raw material procurement, production scheduling, and distribution requirement planning. The interplay between final consumer demand and marketing initiatives (as proposed in the marketing budget) is also evaluated, with the expected impact of these marketing initiatives considered as part of the forecasting process. The interplay between sales quotas and account response is also evaluated, with the expected impact of these quotas considered as part of the forecasting process as well.

New products that enter commercialization almost definitely will be launched, unless a catastrophic event or major shift in company business strategy occurs. As the launch date approaches, the new product becomes part of the S&OP process. In accordance with the traditional S&OP process, the aforementioned baseline forecast, adjusted forecast, and final/approved forecast apply. The S&OP process also mandates that supply chain constraints be discussed. Upon approving and finalizing the new product sales forecast on which launch will be predicated, a launch control protocol should be constructed (see chapter 7). The purpose of a launch control protocol is to foresee potential launch problems, establish launch metrics and tracking signals, and formulate contingency plans for mitigating select launch problems. The following steps are prescribed during the commercialization phase:

C1. *Review and Verify New Product Forecast Assumptions:* Recall and reappraise assumptions established in previous NPD stages. Determine which assumptions remain valid, and which are incorrect or too vague.

C2. *Revise New Product Forecast Assumptions:* Update all assumptions as deemed necessary. Add new assumptions considered important to determining new product sales forecasts from financial and especially unit volume perspectives. The remaining assumptions are deemed the final set of assumptions that will provide the most meaningful new product forecast.

C3. *Generate Baseline Unit Sales Forecast:* Incorporate available data based on the final set of assumptions. Calculate financial and unit volume sales forecasts.

C4. *Adjust Baseline Unit Sales Forecast:* Issue forecasts out to marketing/product management, sales, manufacturing/operations, and finance. Allow each functional area to provide final feedback on the issued forecasts. Through several meetings, this final feedback is reconciled into establishing financial and unit volume sales forecasts.

C5. *Apply Supply Chain Constraints:* Operational issues pertaining to procurement, manufacturing, and distribution are brought out to indicate possible capacity and resource constraints. These constraints are applied to the unit sales forecast to determine feasibility in meeting expected demand within the given budget and financial targets.

C6. *Approve Unit Sales Forecast as Part of the S&OP Process:* The executive S&OP meeting makes final approval on the new product's sales forecast and launch schedule. Product launch is now imminent.

C7. *Construct Launch Control Protocol:* The launch team now assigned to the new product evaluates possible launch problems and contingency plans for mitigating these problems, if they occur. A tracking system, including metrics to be tracked and signals for indicating that a problem exists, is designed. These data comprise the launch control protocol for the new product. The launch scorecard is predicated on the tracking system and issued in conjunction with the final launch schedule.

Postlaunch

Immediately after launch, data are collected and a launch scorecard is periodically issued. Normally, the launch scorecard is issued weekly for the first four to eight weeks, and then presented as part of the executive S&OP meeting on a monthly basis. After six periods (usually six months), new product forecasting transitions over to the regular sales forecasting process. New product forecast accuracy continues to be tracked during the first year and reported during the S&OP reporting process. After the first year forecast accuracy is included with regular tracking of forecast accuracy as part of base business, assuming the new product succeeds.

Should the tracking signal indicate a launch problem, the contingency plan designated in the launch control problem is enacted. Root cause analysis is conducted to document, explain, and share why the problem occurred during the launch postmortem meeting or the executive S&OP meeting.

Assumptions Management

In each of the stages, establishing and revising assumptions is an important, if not a preeminent step across all NPD stages in the course of forecasting new products. Indeed, new product forecasting should be viewed as a process of assumptions management, which entails the generation, translation, and tracking of assumptions.

To generate a new product forecast, a clear set of assumptions should be established, detailed, and documented at the point when the first forecast for the new product is generated. Naturally as the new product forecast is reevaluated through the NPD process, assumptions will be revisited, verified, and reissued to underlie the new product forecast, reduce uncertainty, and instill confidence in the proximate accuracy and meaningfulness of the new product forecast.

A key to assumptions management is tracking, and the launch control protocol mentioned here can be useful in establishing which assumptions should be tracked within the framework of a launch scorecard. The reporting of critical new product assumptions (i.e., within the guise of critical assumptions planning, which will be discussed in chapter 3) should be part of discussions during the S&OP process and the executive S&OP team. Critical assumptions are the most likely candidates for launch tracking and for being a part of the launch scorecard. Common critical assumptions should represent the normal set of tracking metrics for all new product launches and become a normal part of the S&OP launch postmortem discussions. A standardized launch scorecard would be recommended, incorporating those critical assumptions deemed common across NPD projects.

A benefit of assumptions management is the development of a database of critical assumptions and their metrics over time. Once a sizeable database is amassed, analysis can be performed to assess the relationship of various assumptions to new product success and failure. This will further validate whether assumptions can be characterized as critical or not. Analysis can be further applied to developing a model for use in portfolio management, incorporating data for critical assumptions early in the NPD process through technical development. Without a mindset toward new product forecasting as assumptions management, assumptions are not regularly verified or tracked to gauge consistency in the new product forecasting endeavor. Assumptions further reinforce the notion of meaningful forecasting. Failing to manage and track assumptions makes forecasts less meaningful and suspect to company politics because assumptions not documented and not tracked can meander and be easily manipulated.

S&OP and New Product Forecasting

Up to this point, various references have been made to the process known as Sales and Operations Planning (S&OP). In accordance with the work of recognized S&OP expert Thomas Wallace, S&OP is a cross-functional process that links key departments such as Sales, Marketing, Operations, Finance, and Product Development for the purpose of developing an integrated set of plans that all of these departments can support. These recommended plans are presented to the Executive S&OP Team (a cross-functional group consisting of senior level managers) for their approval or a senior management decision to modify the plans. The output of the S&OP process is an authorized company-wide plan for managing the entire business, including production, inventory, materials, sales, marketing, and finance decisions (refer to Wallace 1999). The aim of S&OP is to keep demand and supply in balance by linking the company's strategic plans and business plans to the tactical processes of demand forecasting, order entry, master scheduling, plant scheduling, and purchasing. "Used properly, S&OP enables the company's managers to view the business holistically and gives them a window into the future" (Wallace 1999, p. 7).

It is important to recognize the keen link between new product forecasting and S&OP. Because product development plays a key role in this process, so too must there be a role for new product forecasting. Unfortunately, there is little delineation of this role and the steps to be taken in the course of serving this role. Wallace (1999, p. 99) stated that "new product launch issues need to be visible in all of the S&OP steps: Demand Planning phase, Supply Planning phase, Pre-SOP meeting, and executive S&OP meeting" to specify the impact that the new product has with regards to new demand and supply procedures. "Where practical, the impact of new product launches should be displayed on the S&OP spreadsheets both in the quantitative section of the display and in the Comments section" (Wallace 2000, p. 99).

The discussion from previous sections in this chapter on the new product forecasting process should clarify the steps, details, and thought necessary to manifest meaningful new product forecasting. Figure 2.3 illustrates how the new product forecasting process represents a reconciliation process of multiple inputs and functional forecast perspectives that then represent inputs into the S&OP process.

Key Concepts

New Product Development Process
New Product Teams
New Product Forecasting Process
Sales and Operations Planning Process

Figure 2.3 **New Product Forecasting and the S&OP Process**

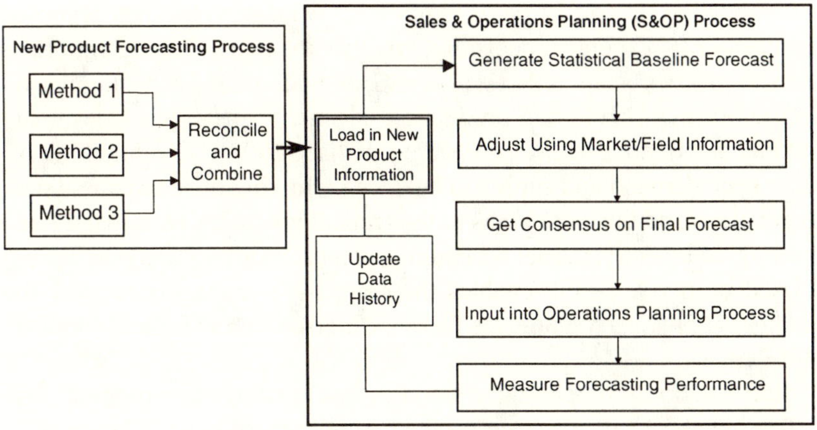

Discussion Questions

1. Why should new product forecasting be considered a process?
2. What are the various stages and gates of the new product development process?
3. What kinds of new product forecasting activities occur during each stage of the typical new product development process?
4. Why should new product forecasting be viewed as a process of assumptions management?
5. How does new product forecasting link to the sales and operations planning process?

Part II

New Product Forecasting Techniques

It is far better to foresee even without
certainty than not to foresee at all.
Henri Poincare, Mathematician (1854–1912)

Once a foundation is established, forecasting techniques may then be applied. Still, one should not tread forward without first being cognizant of the nuances and assumptions that underlie each technique one may plan to use. To help one understand applicable new product forecasting techniques, chapters 3 through 6 discuss the four major categories of forecasting techniques and the guidelines that apply to each of these categories and the techniques found in each respective category. Chapter 3 specifically discusses judgmental techniques, chapter 4 discusses customer and market research techniques, chapter 5 discusses time series techniques, and chapter 6 discusses how regression modeling can be used to forecast new products.

3

Judgmental New Product
Forecasting Techniques

There are a number of judgmental forecasting techniques applicable to the task of new product forecasting available. The objective of these techniques is to turn experience, judgment, and intuition into a formal forecast. While typically easy to initiate, judgmental techniques should not be viewed as always the easiest to implement, particularly in terms of reaching a company consensus on the forecast due to organizational politics. The present chapter discusses the common judgmental techniques of jury of executive opinion, sales force composite, scenario analysis, Delphi method, assumptions-based modeling, decision trees, and Markov process models.

Jury of Executive Opinion

Jury of executive opinion is a top-down forecasting technique where the forecast is arrived at through the ad-hoc combination of opinions and predictions made by informed executives and experts. Empirical analyses also may be used to supplement opinion.

Top-down means that a forecast is made at the highest level and then proportioned accordingly. For example, Figure 3.1 shows a new product's total domestic United States forecast to be 1,000 units. This forecast is proportioned out to lower levels (or "blown down"). As shown, the 1,000-unit forecast is proportioned across geographic regions with 200 units forecast for the Northeast Region, 325 units forecast for the Southeast Region, 250 units forecast for the Midwest Region, and 225 units forecast for the West Region. The forecast can be proportioned down as low

Figure 3.1 **Top-Down Versus Bottom-Up Forecasting**

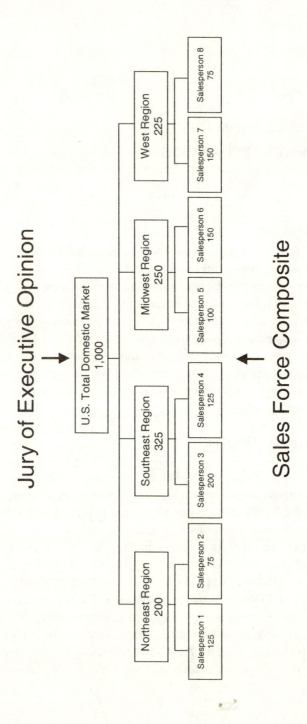

as needed, for example, the account level, the distribution center level, the customer location level, or another lower level. Figure 3.1 illustrates the proportioning down to the individual salesperson level.

Sales Force Composite

A reverse approach to the jury of executive opinion technique is the bottoms-up approach. Here lower-level forecasts are aggregated or "rolled up" to higher levels in the forecasting hierarchy. This approach is often called the sales force composite technique due to the tradition of individual salesperson forecasts being aggregated to suggest a total market forecast. As shown in Figure 3.1, the two salespersons for the Northeast Region when added together suggest a Northeast Region unit volume forecast of 200 units (125 for Salesperson 1 + 75 for Salesperson 2). Summing up the four regions suggests a total domestic forecast of 1,000 units.

Scenario Analysis

Scenario analysis does not normally provide a numeric forecast, contrasting jury of executive opinion and sales force composite techniques, which usually do generate numeric forecasts. The output of scenario analysis is a depiction and description of a future state, thereby characterizing this technique as a narrative forecasting technique.

Two general types of scenario analysis can be employed. The first is the exploratory or extend approach, which uses "seed trends" to establish a current state. "Seed trends" require the forecaster to identify current market characteristics and market trends, and using these data, progress into the future. Future events based on the seed trends are depicted and narrative descriptions of future trends and end states are constructed.

The second approach is the normative or leap approach. Here the forecaster jumps (leaps) out to the future with or without consideration for current trends. A picture of the future state is painted. Two options are then possible. A static leap takes the future narrative description and establishes it as a point of reference and future benchmark. A dynamic leap takes the future narrative description and connects what is proposed to the current state of activities. A roadmap that includes necessary strategies, programs, and actions for getting to the proposed future state from the current state is constructed.

Figure 3.2 **Scenario Analysis**

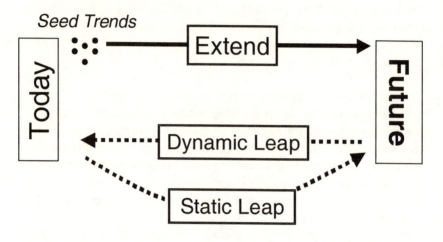

For purposes of illustration, one could use the extend approach to predict future patterns of commuting in light of trends suggesting worse traffic, higher gas prices, the emergence of hybrid (gas and electric) vehicles, and continual improvements in computer and telecommunication technologies. Stepping out, predictions would be made about the state of commuting, say five, ten, or more years into the future. The leap approach might involve brainstorming of likely future commuting states like hydrogen vehicles, telecommuting, Web commuting, and even teleportation. Use of a dynamic leap approach could be employed to connect these future states to current strategies and plans of the company in these or related areas. If the respective company was a computer manufacturer, the type of computer hardware and software to support Web commuting might be taken into consideration and compared against the current portfolio of product and service offerings. Any apparent gaps in the portfolio would be discussed and documented. Figure 3.2 illustrates the scenario analysis technique.

Delphi Method

The Delphi method is a group decision-making approach that is designed to gather subjective expert opinion through structured anonymous rounds of data collection. Each successive round provides consolidated feedback to the respondents so that the forecast can be further refined and consensus on the forecast reached. The overriding objective of the Delphi method is to capture the advantages of multiple experts in a committee, while minimizing the effects of social pressure to agree with the majority, ego pressure to stick with your original forecast despite new information, the influence of a repetitive argument, or the influence of a dominant individual.

Variations of the Delphi technique exist, but generally there is a forecast coordinator who serves as the repository of forecast information. The forecast coordinator selects and queries the experts who will serve as the respondent committee base. To minimize any bias in the forecasting effort, confidentiality of the expert is maintained by the forecast coordinator so no one else knows the identities of the expert panel aside from the forecast coordinator. Some computer software can ensure complete anonymity.

Two types of forecasting information are collected. First is the forecast itself, usually in a numeric form. The second type of information is the rationale behind the forecast. The forecast coordinator takes these data, and when all experts have submitted their responses, sends all the forecasts and their rationales back out to the expert panel in no particular order to ensure confidentiality. The experts then evaluate the forecasts and their rationales, and are asked if they would like to revise their forecasts. The goal is to work toward and achieve consensus on the forecast. To do this, multiple rounds of receiving and sending forecast information are likely necessary.

The key benefit of the Delphi approach versus other forecasting techniques is the presence of both a numeric forecast and a narrative rationale for why the forecast is what it is. That way, there is an express understanding that underlies the forecast, versus simply just a number. While appealing, the Delphi approach is not normally a fast forecasting technique because multiple query rounds are usually necessary. The Delphi approach may take several days or even weeks to complete, depending on the given forecasting task. Another issue in using the Delphi approach is the effect of anchoring, which occurs when experts fix on their own forecast and are not agreeable to consensus. Anchoring results in two or more distinct forecasts emerging, which is not necessarily bad because it paints multiple outcomes along with a rationale for why they may come to fruition. The problem that anchoring presents, though, is how to reconcile distinctly different forecasts. One could simply average the numeric forecasts or take a weighted average of the numeric

Figure 3.3 **Delphi Approach**

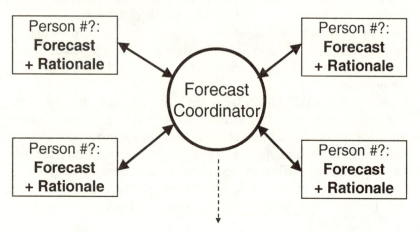

Goal = Consensus on the "Forecast"

forecasts. Historical forecast accuracy of each individual expert could be employed as the basis for calculating the respective weighting factors. Figure 3.3 illustrates the Delphi approach.

Assumptions-Based Modeling

Assumptions-based modeling is a technique that attempts to model the behavior of the relevant market environment by breaking the market behavior into individual components. Values for these components (also called market drivers) are determined (assumed) and forecasts are generated. Other names for assumptions-based models include chain models and market breakdown models.

An illustration of the assumptions-based modeling framework is presented in Figure 3.4. As shown, modeling begins with the potential target market size. This highlights the importance of carefully articulating, identifying, and detailing the intended target market before beginning the new product forecasting endeavor and prior to specifying other key market drivers. The potential target market is subsequently proportioned down to the available target market, then to the qualified target market, then to the attainable target market, and finally, to the penetrated target market. Numerous variations of this breakdown framework are possible, depending on the assumptions of the company and the forecaster.

Figure 3.4 **An Assumptions-Based Modeling Framework**

An assumptions-based modeling framework commonly used in the consumer packaged goods industry is the ATAR model (see Figure 3.5). ATAR stands for awareness, trial, availability, and repeat purchase and is predicated on the hierarchy of effects model (see Kahn 2000; Crawford and Di Benedetto 2003). As presented in Figure 3.5, the ATAR model begins with the potential target market size and uses the ATAR components to break down the target market size proportionally. The awareness factor breaks down the potential target market size to suggest the magnitude of those who are aware of the new product. Those that are aware are then proportioned down to those that are aware and willing to try the new product. Those that are aware and willing to try the new product are proportioned down to those that are aware, willing to try, and able to get availability of the new product. At this point, potential target market × awareness × trial × availability provides an initial trial market size, assuming that customers buy only one trial. In other words, a model based on just potential target market × awareness × trial × availability provides an estimate of the likely sales jump due to customers becoming aware, deciding to try, and actively going out to buy the new product for the first time.

Adding the components of repeat and number bought per period estimates the expected repeat sales rate. The repeat purchase rate would

Figure 3.5 **The ATAR Model**

Profit = Units Sold x Profit Per Unit

Units Sold (Initial Trial) = # of Buying Units x % Awareness x % Trial x % Availability

Units Sold (Repeat Model) = # of Buying Units x % Awareness x % Trial x % Availability x % Repeat x # Repeat Purchases

Revenue Per Unit - Cost Per Unit = **Profit Per Unit**

represent the percent of those who are aware, willing to try, are able to get availability, and who wish to buy again. This estimate is multiplied by the number of purchases expected in a given period (e.g., month, quarter, year) to calculate the total new product volume resulting from repeat purchases. Adding together the resulting figure from the initial trail market size model and the figure from the repeat rate market size model generates a total volume estimate for a new product during the given period (typically annually).

One limitation of the ATAR model is an explicit omission of competition. Thus, the output of the ATAR model is more akin to a sales potential estimate, depending on the assumptions employed in the model. The forecaster may choose to reduce the model's estimates by a desired or necessary-to-attain market share/penetration rate, which would more closely reflect a sales forecast. Including a market share/penetration rate reflects the fact that rarely does 100 percent of the market immediately buy a new product. Relying on innovation research (cf. Rogers 1995), five particular market segments can be identified with respect to market adoption of a new product: lead users comprise about 3.5 percent of a market and are first to buy the new product; early adopters comprise 12.5 percent of the market and are second to buy the new product; the early majority makes up 34 percent of the market and is third to buy the new product; the late majority makes up 34 percent of the market and is fourth to buy the new product; and laggards comprise the remaining 16 percent of market and are last to buy the new product (also refer to chapter 7). The forecaster can predict which groups will initially respond to the new product, and using the given percentages, calculate an expected sale volume. For example, if the new product will immediately appeal to lead users, early adopters, and about half of the early majority during the first year of its sales, an esti-mated penetration rate is 33 percent.

Adopting the ATAR Model to the Business-to-Business Context

The ATAR model is a flexible framework and can be fashioned to serve other industries besides consumer packaged goods. If the new product does not lend itself to frequent period repeat purchases as in the case of automobiles, major home appliances, and industrial equipment, then the repeat purchase rate and number bought components can be removed. Components of the ATAR model also can be modified to match key assumptions within a particular industry. For example, Thomas (1993) presents a variation of the ATAR model in the course of forecasting high-definition television (HDTV) sales. The model comprises the com-ponents of population, technology acceptance, awareness, availability, and intention-to-buy factors to estimate market potential. Another ex-ample is the common use of assumptions-based models in the pharma-ceutical industry. The potential target market size is represented by the population size with a particular medical condition. This number then is proportioned down by those who get diagnosed, then proportioned by those who receive a prescription for a given brand, then proportioned by those who actually fill their prescription, and then proportioned by the respective brand's channel availability.

Company management should stress that a common, consistent as-sumptions modeling framework be used so that forecasts can be com-pared on an equal basis. While an individual forecaster controls the composition of the assumptions-based model, the use of common model components allows for standardized discussion during gate reviews. Common model components also facilitate the tracking and evaluation of model components when the new product is eventually launched be-cause a launch scorecard can be standardized across all new products (also refer to chapter 7).

The Ship-Share Model

Some consumer packaged goods (CPG) companies use a ship-share model to forecast new products along with existing products. The ship-share model is a type of assumptions-based model incorporating the following three assumption components: how much inventory will go into the trade supply pipeline (beginning retail inventory), how much product will consumers take away (consumer takeaway), and how much inventory will retailers hold (expected ending retail inventory). Estimating these assumptions, factory shipments can be forecast using the formula below:

Beginning Retail Inventory Level – Consumer Takeaway +
Factory Shipments = Ending Retail Inventory Level

For purposes of illustration, let us assume that the marketing department expects the Beginning Retail Inventory to be 400,000 units based on supply pipeline preshipments. The new product is expected to grow the current market by 7 percent and the current company unit market share is 6.8 percent. Monthly category unit sales are currently 1,625,000 units so the expected monthly consumer takeaway is 118,235 units $(1,625,000 \times 1.07 \times .068)$. On average, retailers hold about three months supply, but it is expected that retailers plan to decrease their inventories by 6 percent. The ending retail inventory is calculated to be 333,423 units $(118,235 \times 3 \times .94)$. Using the formula, factory shipments are calculated as follows: $400,000 - 118,235 +$ Factory Shipments $= 333,423$ or factory shipments equal $333,423 - 281,765$ or $51,658$ units. In this way, factory shipments are used to balance the equation. Figure 3.6 visualizes this example of the ship-share model.

Akin to all assumptions-based models, the precision of ship-share models is suspect due to the compounding of multiple assumptions. Ship-share models and assumptions-based models are therefore better suited for general estimation and directional purposes in the course of establishing a baseline forecast. The components of the ship-share model also should be tracked to validate whether each component is coming to fruition as predicted.

NPD Process Evaluation: The Decay Curve and Expenditures Curve

Another variation of assumptions-based modeling is in the use of evaluating the new product development (NPD) process through the forecasting of risk, cost, and time dimensions. In the course of this evaluative analysis, two evaluations tools called the decay curve (mortality curve) and the expenditures curve can be developed and subsequently employed.

Figure 3.6 **An Example of a Ship-Share Model**

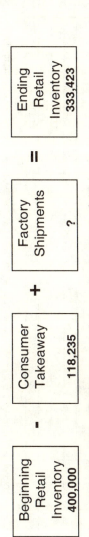

| Beginning Retail Inventory 400,000 | − | Consumer Takeaway 118,235 | + | Factory Shipments ? | = | Ending Retail Inventory 333,423 |

We know Beginning Retail Inventory = 400,000 units

We estimate Consumer Takeaway = 118,235 units
❖ Total Retail Unit Market Growth is 7%
❖ Company Unit Market Share is 6.8%

Category Unit Sales x 1.07 x .068 = 1,625,000 x 1.07 x .068 = 118,235 units

We estimate Ending Retail Inventory = 333,423 units
❖ Retailers plan to decrease inventories 6% per month

Prior Month Supply (3.0 months) x .94 = 2.7 months supply
118,235 x 2.7 = 333,423 units

Factory Shipments = 51,658 units

50

Figure 3.7 **Evaluating the NPD Process**

NPD Stage	Risk	Cost	Time	No. of Ideas Needed
CG	0.50	$700,000	5	7.71
PTE	0.57	$4,100,000	6	3.86
TD	0.70	$2,600,000	12	2.20
C	0.65	$5,900,000	4	1.54
Totals		$13,300,000	27	1.00
		Probability of 1 Success =		0.1297
		# of Ideas Needed for Success =		7.71

NPD Stage	No. of Ideas	Cost Considerations			Time Considerations		
		Expected Cost	Percent of Total	Cumulative Percentage	Expected Time	Percent of Total	Cumulative Percentage
CG	7.71	$5,398,111	15%	15%	38.56	41%	41%
PTE	3.86	$15,808,753	44%	59%	23.13	25%	65%
TD	2.20	$5,714,286	16%	75%	26.37	28%	93%
C	1.54	$9,076,923	25%	100%	6.15	7%	100%
Total		$35,998,072			94.22		
One-Shot Totals		$102,564,103			208.21		
Difference		–$66,566,030			–113.99		

Note: CG = concept generation; PTE = pretechnical evaluation; TD = technical development; C = commercialization.

Figure 3.7 portrays a four-stage NPD process with data for risk, cost, and time dimensions. Risk is defined as the percent of product concepts that successfully make it through a given stage (i.e., successfully pass the respective stage's gate review). Cost is defined as the standard cost for one product concept to progress through the given stage. And time is defined as the standard time for one product concept to progress through the given stage. As shown, each product concept has a 50 percent chance of surviving the concept generation stage at a cost of $700,000 per concept and a time consumption of five person-weeks per concept. Each product concept has a 57 percent of surviving the pretechnical evaluation stage at a cost of $1,400,000 per concept and a time consumption of six person-weeks per concept. A product concept entering the technical development stage has a 70 percent chance of survival at a cost of $2,600,000 per concept and a time consumption of twelve person-weeks. The final stage of product development reflects a 65 percent chance of traversing the commercialization stage at a cost of $5,900,000 and a time consumption of four person-weeks.

Multiplying the risk data across the four NPD stages calculates the overall risk of one concept successfully traversing NPD stages from concept generation through product launch. Based on the data in Figure 3.6, there is about a 13 percent "success" rate ($.50 \times .57 \times .70 \times .65 = 13\%$). The reciprocal of this probability suggests the number of concepts necessary to launch one "successful" product, assuming that the NPD process funnels concepts in accordance with the given percentages. The given data suggests that 7.71 ideas or roughly 8 ideas are needed to result in one product launch. Taking the number of ideas needed and multiplying by risk per stage calculates the number of concepts needed per NPD stages. As suggested, 7.71 concepts are needed at the beginning of the start of the concept generation stage, 3.86 concepts are needed at the beginning of the pretechnical evaluation stage ($7.71 \times .50 = 3.86$), 2.20 concepts are needed at the beginning of the technical development stage ($3.86 \times .57 = 2.20$), and 1.54 concepts are needed at the beginning of the commercialization stage ($2.20 \times .70 = 1.54$). Graphing these data points constructs what is called the "decay curve" (also referred to as the "mortality curve") as presented in Figure 3.8. The decay curve is a representation of the "funneling effect" that the NPD process reflects and suggests how stringent the product development process is in reducing the total sample of product concepts to eventually launch one product. Between the two general regions found on the decay curve,

Figure 3.8 **The Decay Curve**

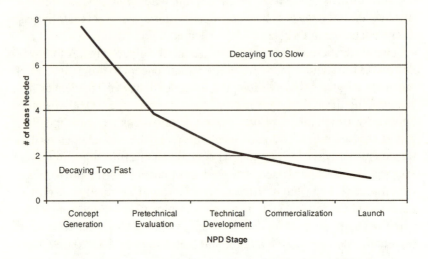

the area above the curve indicates a "slow decay," which is a situation where product concepts are not necessarily being eliminated as they should be. A product development project team staying above the curve suggests that the project team is allowing too many product concepts through the process and will have too many product concepts at the end of the process. The area below the curve indicates a "fast decay," which is a situation where many product concepts are being eliminated. A product development project team staying below the curve suggests that the project team does not have enough product concepts to sustain the product development process and will not have a single product to launch. A product development project team staying near the company's decay curve would closely approximate the expected product development process for the respective company.

The decay curve also can be used as a benchmark for comparison with industry decay curves. The Product Development and Management Association (PDMA) surveys companies about every five years to establish industry NPD decay rates. Results of the PDMA 2003 Comparative Performance Assessment Study (CPAS) suggest an industry development success rate of 22 percent, which requires about five product concepts to ensure one successfully launched product. The idea screening stage has a 64 percent success rate, the business analysis stage has a

68 percent success rate, the technical development stage has a 72 percent success rate, the test and validation stage has an 85 percent success rate, and the commercialization stage has an 84 percent success rate (Adams-Bigelow 2004).

Using these product concept counts, cost and time data can be used to estimate budget and schedule requirements associated with each NPD stage, and subsequently, estimate the totals for budget and schedule for the overall NPD process. With the example shown in Figure 3.7, the concept generation stage will optimally evaluate 7.71 concepts a stage cost of $700,000 per concept and a time factor of five person-weeks per concept. The cost of the concept generation stage is calculated to be $5,398,111 (7.71 × $700,000) and take 38.56 people-weeks to complete fully (7.71 × 5 people-weeks). In a similar fashion, the pretechnical evaluation stage will cost $15,808,753 and take 23.13 person-weeks; the technical development stage will cost $5,714,286 and take 26.37 person-weeks; and the commercialization stage will cost $9,076,923 and take 6.15 weeks to complete. Summing this data provides a budget forecast for financial and human resources. Specifically, the analysis suggests that a budget of $35,998,072 and 94.22 person-weeks will be needed to develop and launch one product. If more than one product is desired, these figures serve as multiplicative factors. For example, a goal of five product launches will require a financial budget of $179,990,360 (5 × $35,998,072) and human resources of 472.75 person weeks (5 × 94.22).

Calculating the relative and cumulative percentages for cost and time dimensions across each NPD stage provides additional insight. As shown in Figure 3.7, the costliest product development stage is pretechnical evaluation, which accounts for 44 percent of the total project costs in the course of developing and launching a new product. The most time-consuming stage is concept generation, which accounts for 41 percent of total project time to develop and launch one product. The cumulative percentages indicate that almost 60 percent of project costs are expensed after completing the pretechnical evaluation stage, while 65 percent of project time is consumed following completion of the pretechnical evaluation stage. Comparing cumulative percentage data graphically creates the "expenditures curve," which shows the cumulative percentage of cost versus the cumulative percent of time (refer to Figure 3.9). This curve is useful as an internal company benchmark to evaluate NPD projects and determine if costs are running high versus time. The expenditures curve has two predominant regions, akin to the decay curve. A

Figure 3.9 **The Expenditures Curve**

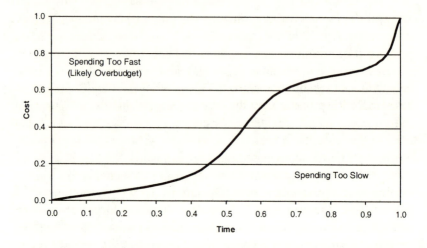

project found above the curve would suggest an overbudget situation (the budget is being spent too quickly). A project below the curve would suggest an underbudget situation, possibly suggesting that resources are not being expensed as intended (which could be good or bad). A project falling close to the derived curve would be within normal expected company NPD spending and schedule parameters.

Using Assumptions-Based Models to Identify Critical Assumptions and Examine Risk

The overall reliability and validity of assumptions-based models are predicated on the individual reliability and validity of each assumption inputted. This is one limitation when employing assumptions-based models because an uneducated, wild guess on a particular assumption will almost always result in an erroneous new product forecast.

Precision is another limitation. Slight deviations in the percentages surrounding assumptions can result in significant swings in the resulting new product forecast. Because of such sensitivity to slight deviations in inputs, assumptions-based models are suited for general estimation and directional purposes in the course of establishing a baseline forecast. Yet, if the goal is to derive a new product forecast (as is the case in many companies), a range of inputs should be used to portray pessimistic, likely, and optimistic cases in the course of what-if analysis, thereby generating a possible range of outcomes. The analyst using this approach can determine if the range of outcomes is acceptable within given company parameters. If not, further thinking is imperative to determine what needs to happen (that is, what does the company need to do in terms of strategy and tactics) to make the range fall within acceptable boundaries. This exemplifies how assumptions-based models are used as tools for what-if scenario analysis and sensitivity analyses to establish critical assumptions as well as examine pending risk.

This focuses attention on the model components themselves, and thus, there is the need to understand the variability expected across each of the model components and how fluctuations in each of the components will influence the new product forecast estimate. Inputting pessimistic, likely, and optimistic values for each assumption will allow a sensitivity analysis to be performed on each model component in order to isolate those model components that have the propensity to force a negative revenue stream, for example. Those model components with pessimistic values forcing a negatively viewed outcome would be deemed critical and referred to as critical assumptions.

The delineation of critical assumptions can help in directing proper market research. Such research can be useful in gauging variability around a particular critical assumption and tightening the uncertainty surrounding that assumption. Better understanding of critical assumptions is essential to achieving an understanding and a more accurate market forecast.

Consider the financial assumptions-model shown in Table 3.1. This model, which was constructed to forecast a new computer technology, includes the components of total market size, the percent of the marketplace using the new technology as core technology (the intended, marketed use), company market share in the core technology use segment, buying intent (the percent of the market interested and likely ready to migrate to the new core technology), and company market coverage. The total market size is $3,000,000,000 accompanied by pessimistic, likely (base case), and optimistic values for the remaining assumptions. (Refer to Table 3.1.)

The likely case (also called the base case) predicts that revenue will be $89,250,000 ($3,100,000,000 × .40 × .10 × .20 × .80). A risk management methodology is then applied by holding all values constant and changing one value to its pessimistic and optimistic cases. This allows

Table 3.1

Pessimistic, Likely, and Optimistic Values for a Given Assumptions-Based Model

	Pessimistic case	Likely case (base case)	Optimistic case
Market size	$3,000,000,000	$3,000,000,000	$3,000,000,000
Percent core use	0.70	0.40	0.80
Market share	0.20	0.10	0.30
Buying intent	0.25	0.20	0.30
Market coverage	0.85	0.80	0.95

Assumptions-Based Model Equation:
$ Sales = Market Size × % Core Use × % Market Share × % Buying Intent × % Market Coverage

Table 3.2

An Example of Model Sensitivity with Regard to Financial Outcome

	Pessimistic case	Optimistic case	Likely case (base case)
Percent core use	$51,000,000	$102,000,000	$89,250,000
Market share	$44,625,000	$133,875,000	$89,250,000
Buying intent	$71,400,000	$107,100,000	$89,250,000
Market coverage	$84,000,000	$ 99,750,000	$89,250,000

for an assessment of the model's sensitivity to each case assumption. Model sensitivity with regard to financial outcome is also assessed, as shown in Table 3.2.

Subtracting the pessimistic case from the likely case on each component suggests the potential shortfall that would result if the respective pessimistic case came to fruition. Subtracting the likely case from the optimistic case on each component suggests the potential upside from the base case that would result if the respective optimistic case came to fruition. Adding these values indicates an overall sensitivity of the model to that respective component. These values also can be graphed in the form of a Tornado chart, which sorts the largest fluctuating component to the smallest fluctuating component, thereby highlighting which components contribute the greatest risk (cf. Clemen 1997). Further study of those components deemed riskiest will highlight high potential risk situations. (Refer to Table 3.3 and Figure 3.10.)

Table 3.3

An Example of Evaluating Potential Shortfall, Upside, and Total Risk

	Potential shortfall from the base case if the pessimistic case were to occur	Potential upside from the base case if the optimistic case were to occur	Potential risk (in terms of financial revenue range)
Percent core use	−$38,250,000	$12,750,000	$51,000,000
Market share	−$44,625,000	$44,625,000	$89,250,000
Buying intent	−$17,850,000	$17,850,000	$35,700,000
Market coverage	−$ 5,250,000	$10,500,000	$15,750,000

Assumptions-based models can be readily adapted to the use of business simulation by simulating values of the inputted assumptions. For example, use of the @RAND function in Microsoft Excel can be used to randomly select values between the pessimistic and optimistic cases on each assumption (note that the @RAND function uses a uniform distribution from which to pull random numbers; other distributions can be modeled as well, cf. Weida, Richardson, and Vazonyi 2001). As shown in Table 3.4, five separate simulation runs present five different sets of assumptions. By running 100 or more simulations, one can begin to see a distribution of risk for the outcome, in this case the revenue forecast, and probabilities of being below and above the base case can be ascertained. For example, Figure 3.11 presents the results of a 100-run simulation. These results show that there is a 32 percent chance of being above the $90,000,000, which is slightly above the base case, and infer that management attachment and commitment to the base case of $89,250,000 for the new product forecast may not be advisable (in other words, there is an approximate 67 percent chance of falling below the base case). The simulation results therefore suggest that the base case may be more optimistic than intended and that further analysis and discussion are warranted.

Decision Trees

Decision trees generate a numeric new product forecast using probabilities that are connected to particular courses of action. These probabilities are usually determined in a subjective fashion, and an expected value of occurrence is calculated using conditional probabilities for each course of action (events). The example in Figure 3.12 shows a tree diagram of two scenarios under consideration: option A requires an investment of

58

Figure 3.10 **A Tornado Chart**

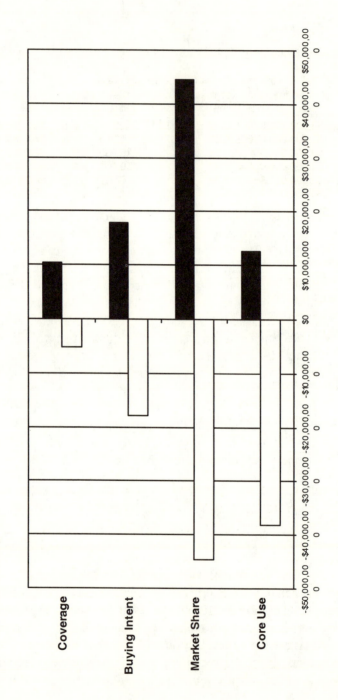

Table 3.4

An Example of Simulation Data Using the @Rand Function in Microsoft® Excel

	Market size (constant)	Percent core use	Market share	Buying intent	Market coverage	Financial revenue
Base case	$3,000,000,000	0.70	0.20	0.25	0.95	$89,250,000
Run 1	$3,000,000,000	0.43	0.15	0.22	0.91	$40,454,556
Run 2	$3,000,000,000	0.74	0.13	0.26	0.83	$64,462,989
Run 3	$3,000,000,000	0.57	0.26	0.24	0.89	$94,740,045
Run 4	$3,000,000,000	0.69	0.15	0.21	0.91	$60,113,354
Run 5	$3,000,000,000	0.47	0.25	0.26	0.91	$85,676,052
. . .	. . .	. . .	. . .	. . .	. . .	. . .

$20 million, and option B requires an investment of $40 million. Option A has two revenue scenarios: there is the lower-revenue option of $15 million with a probability of .30, and the higher-revenue option of $25 million with a probability of .7. Option B has three revenue scenarios: there is a lower-revenue option of $20 million with a probability of .4, the medium-revenue option of $40 million with a probability of .4, and the higher-revenue option of $80 million with a probability of .20. The conditional probabilities for each lowest-level scenario are first multiplied with their respective corresponding outcomes to calculate an expected return per decision. The two revenue scenarios of option A reflect an expected return of $4.5 million ($15 million × .30) for the lower-revenue option and an expected return of $17.5 million ($25 million × .7) for the higher-revenue option. The three revenue scenarios of option B reflect an expected return of $8 million ($20 million × .4) for the lower-revenue option, an expected return of $16 million ($40 million × .4) for the medium-revenue option, and an expected return of $16 million ($80 million × .2) for the higher-revenue option. Adding the values for each option and then subtracting the suggested cost for each option forecasts an overall expected return per option. Option A reflects an expected return of $2 million, which equals $4.5 million + $17.5 million – $20 million. Option B reflects an expected return of $0 million, which equals $8 million + $16 million + $16 million – $40 million. Based on the forecast analysis, option A is shown to be the more attractive option because the expected revenue forecast of $2 million is certainly more attractive than the expected no revenue forecast in the case of option B.

Figure 3.11 Graphing Results from a Simulation of 100 Runs

Figure 3.12 The Decision Tree Methodology

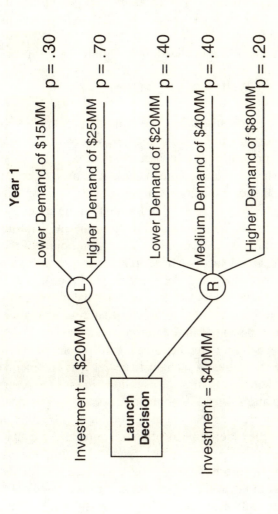

Year 1

Lower Demand of $15MM   p = .30

Higher Demand of $25MM   p = .70

L   Investment = $20MM

Lower Demand of $20MM   p = .40

Medium Demand of $40MM   p = .40

Higher Demand of $80MM   p = .20

R   Investment = $40MM

Launch Decision

Expected Return After Year 1

E(Local Option) = (.30 × $15MM) + (.70 × $25MM) − $20MM = $22MM − $20MM = **$2 million**

E(Regional Option) = (.40 × $20MM) + (.40 × $40MM) + (.20 × $80MM) − $40MM = $40MM − $40MM = **$0**

ECV Model

A variation of the decision tree approach is the expected commercial value (ECV) model (Cooper, Edgett, and Kleinschmidt 1998). This model discounts future revenue by the probability of commercial success and the probability of technical success, along with the consideration of commercialization costs and development costs. Used in the course of new product portfolio management, the ECV model calculates an expected commercial value for individual NPD projects. ECV is then used in the decision-making process to determine which projects should move forward.

The ECV model is operationalized by the following formula:

$$ECV = [(NPV \times P_{cs} - C) \times P_{ts} - D]$$

where ECV is the expected commercial value of the product concept, NPV is the net present value of the product concept's future earnings discounted to the present, P_{cs} is the probability of commercial success (given technical success), C is commercialization costs, P_{ts} is the probability of technical success, and D is development costs (remaining in the project). Figure 3.13 presents this formula within a decision tree framework. Akin to assumptions-based models, the ECV formula can be modified to reflect more than the two decision points of technical success and commercial success, if desired. As shown in Figure 3.13, product concepts A and B are underconsidered, with project A reflecting the higher ECV even though it does not have the highest NPV. This illustrates how the probabilities of technical success and commercial success can impact the consideration of product concepts.

Akin to the decision tree methodology, care should be taken when estimating the probabilities of technical success and commercial success. Inaccurate estimates of these probabilities will lead to a very erroneous ECV calculation. The ECV approach also suffers from penalizing riskier projects versus ones that are more certain (greater likelihood of success), even when riskier projects often offer greater financial return. The latter can bias decisions on the new product portfolio management in favor of less-risk projects, which, in turn, will lead to an unbalanced new product portfolio that ill-prepares the company strategically.

Cooper, Edgett, and Kleinschmidt (1998) stress that a systematic approach to estimating probability inputs will lead to a better estimate

Figure 3.13 **The Expected Commercial Value (ECV) Methodology**

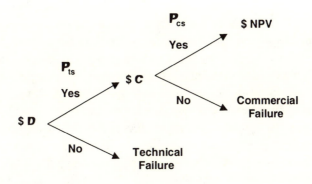

$ ECV = [(NPV x P_{cs} - C) x P_{ts} - D]
Where
$ ECV = Expected commercial value of the project
$ D = Development costs remaining in the project
P_{ts} = Probability of technical success
$ C = Commercialization (launch) costs
P_{cs} = Probability of commercial success
$ NPV = Net present value of the project's future earnings

Project	NPV	P_{ts}	P_{cs}	$ D	$ C	ECV
a	50	0.6	0.75	5	3	15.7
b	66.25	0.5	0.8	10	2	15.5

versus a guess. They suggest that probability estimates can be systematically determined using a Delphi forecasting methodology, a standardized matrix that prespecifies which probabilities to use, or a standard scorecard that derives the probabilities estimates. All said, the sensitivity to input estimates suggest that the decision tree methodology should represent more of a directional forecast versus a precise numeric target.

Markov Process Model

Markov process models are probabilistic frameworks that determine a future state based on current state behavior. Each individual Markov process model contains a matrix of transition rates suggesting the probability of one state being followed by another particular one. The basic assumption of a Markov process model is that the behavior of the system in each state is memoryless; that is, going from the current state to the future state is only determined by what happens in the present state and not by events that have occurred prior to the current state. Within the context of new product forecasting, Markov process models have been employed to forecast consumers' brand-switching behavior among products, allowing for ultimate calculations of market share for products in the given marketplace (see Lilien and Rangaswamy 1998).

Figure 3.14 presents a Markov process model for two competing products called Product A and Product B. The data in the model present customers' purchase behavior among the competing brands X and Y, where 60 percent of consumers who bought Product A will buy Product A again, 40 percent of consumers who bought Product A will buy Product B, 30 percent of consumers who bought Product B will buy Product A, and 70 percent of consumers who bought Product B will buy Product B again. The diagonal of this matrix running from the top left to the lower right indicates brand loyalty among consumers; that is, percent of consumers who bought a particular brand and will buy that brand again. Another way to read the data in the matrix is to consider the columns as the percent of customers gained from a specified competitor and the rows as the percent of customers lost to a specified competitor. For example, the column data indicates that Product A gains 60 percent of its own sales (keeps 60 percent of its sales) and gains 30 percent of sales from Product B, while Product B gains 40 percent of sales from Product A and gains 70 percent of its own sales. The row data indicates that Product A loses 60 percent of its sales to itself (keeps 60 percent of its sales) and loses 40 percent of sales to Product B, while Product B loses 30 percent of sales to Product A and loses 70 percent of its own sales (keeps 70 percent of its sales). Note that each row adds up to 100 percent.

Multiplying the data in the Markov process model by current market share data will forecast future market shares for the two products. For example, initially Product A has a 45 percent market share and Product B has a 55 percent market share. After the next purchase iteration, the market share for Product A will decrease to 43.5 percent, calculated by formulating that Product A gains 60 percent of its 45 percent market share and gains 30 percent of Product B's 55 percent market share [$(.6 \times .45) + (.3 \times .55) = 43.5\%$]. Product B's new market share is 56.5 percent, calculated similarly: Product B gains 40 percent of Product A's 45 percent market share and gains 70 percent of its 55 percent market share

Figure 3.14 **Example of a Markov Process Model**

		$t + 1$	
		Brand A	Brand B
t	Brand A	.55	.45
	Brand B	.50	.50

Initial Market Share
Brand A = 55%
Brand B = 45%

Market Share After Next Purchase Iteration ($t + 1$)

A's Share = (.55 x .55) + (.50 x .45) = 52.75%
B's Share = (.45 x .55) + (.50 x .45) = 47.25%

Market Share After Next Purchase Iteration ($t + 2$)

A's Share = (.55 x .5275) + (.50 x .4725) = 52.64%
B's Share = (.45 x .5275) + (.50 x .4725) = 47.36%

[(.4 × .45) + (.7 × .55) = 56.5%]. Another iteration to calculate future market share would use the newly calculated market shares. After a second purchase iteration, Product A's market share would be 43 percent [(.6 × .435) + (.3 × .565) = 43%], and Product B's market share would be 57 percent [(.4 × .435) + (.7 × .565) = 57%]. Total market share will always add up to 100 percent.

Proceeding through a number of iterations, market share estimates will hone in on a particular value called the "market share steady state." In lieu of making a number of calculations, matrix data can be organized into a set of simultaneous equations and solved to estimate the long-run or "steady state" market shares for each product. With two products under consideration, three equations are formulated. Product A's market share is equal to 60 percent of its own share plus 30 percent of Product B's share, corresponding to the formula .6A + .3B = A; Product B's market share is equal to 40 percent of Product A's share plus 70 percent of its own share, corresponding to the formula .4A + .7B = B; and the sum of the market shares for Products A and B equal 100 percent, corresponding to the formula A + B = 1. Solving for A and B determines that Product A's market share will eventually become 42.9 percent, and Product B's market share will eventually become 57.1 percent. (Refer to Figure 3.15.)

Figure 3.15 **Calculating Steady-State Market Shares Using a Markov Process Model**

		$t + 1$	
		Brand A	Brand B
t	Brand A	.55	.45
	Brand B	.50	.50

Long-Run Market Share
$$A = .55A + .50B$$
$$B = .45A + .50B$$
$$A + B = 1$$

Long-Run Market Share Calculations
$$B = 1 - A$$
$$A = .55A + .50(1 - A)$$
$$A = .55A + .50 - .50A$$
$$.95A = .50$$
$$A = 52.63\% \quad B = 1 - A = 1 - .5263 = 47.37\%$$

Use of Markov process models assumes that the brand-switching probabilities among the given products will remain fairly constant. This assumption may or may not apply given the degree of marketing initiatives being employed by a company and its competitors. While constant probabilities may not be overly realistic, the modeling brand-switching behavior can be a useful what-if financial analysis tool in determining whether a marketing program is cost-effective. Given the prior data example, if every 1 percent of market share represents $100,000 profit, is it worthwhile to spend $250,000 to launch a new product that is presumed to increase Product A's brand loyalty by 5 percent? That is, is it worth $250,000 to increase Product A's gain of its own market share to 65 percent and reduce the loss to Product B to 35 percent? Calculations determine that a 5 percent increase in brand loyalty will increase Product A's long-run market share to 46.2 percent, a 3.3 percent increase from the previous market share of 42.9 percent. The new campaign therefore would conceivably generate $330,000 in profit (3.3 × $100,000) and sufficiently cover the $250,000 budget. The campaign appears worthwhile to implement.

Like the other judgmental techniques previously discussed, a Markov process model is quite useful as a directional decision-making tool, versus a tool for calculating specific numeric targets due to the difficulty in establishing precise brand-switch probabilities and initial market share estimates. Switching data can be calculated based on actual purchase records of former/similar products, customer surveys about previous brand and current brand purchases, expert opinion derived using a Delphi methodology, or subjectively derived from what-if analysis. Markov process models also can be readily employed in conjunction with the ATAR model, where the Markov process model calculates repeat purchase behavior, market share, and cannibalization impacts (the likelihood of the new product taking sales from other company products). Refer to Lilien, Rangaswamy, and Van den Bulte (1999).

Key Concepts

Judgmental Forecasting
Jury of Executive Opinion Technique
Sales Force Composite Technique
Scenario Analysis
Delphi Method
Assumptions-Based Modeling
Critical Assumptions and Risk
Decision Trees
Markov Process Model

Discussion Questions

1. What is a judgmental forecasting technique?
2. What is a top-down forecasting technique? What is a bottom-up forecasting technique?
3. What are the two types of scenario analysis and how do they differ?
4. What are possible benefits and problems when using the Delphi method to forecast new products?
5. What is the premise of assumptions-based modeling?
6. What is a critical assumption? How can one determine whether an assumption is critical?
7. Is it possible to combine multiple judgmental forecasting techniques when forecasting a new product? Why or why not?

4

Customer/Market Research Techniques for New Product Forecasting

New product forecasting should not rely solely on internal sources and company personnel judgment. If possible, external sources both in terms of data and judgment should be canvassed, especially data and judgments from current and potential customers. Such customer data and judgments can be used to clarify assumptions, especially those inputted into a company's assumptions-based model like awareness, trial, repeat purchase, and usage rates.

Three different types of testing may occur with customers throughout the new product development (NPD) process, depending on the form of the product and the testing objective sought. Concept testing, product use testing, and market testing are distinct classes of methodologies that collect, analyze, and interpret customer data in the course of developing new products and making forecasts. Along with these testing forms, the popular methodologies of conjoint analysis and quality function deployment are discussed. Subsumed within quality function deployment are voice-of-the-customer, voice-of-the-engineer, and Kano model analyses, each of which helps to organize thinking around new product functionality and forecasting decisions.

Concept Testing

Early in the NPD process concept testing is performed to proof concepts under consideration and determine those concepts that customers find most favorable. Four types of concept testing can be used, often in tandem with each other. The first type is the narrative statement, which consists of providing customers a written product description on a respective product concept that customers evaluate. The second type is pictorial, which is when the customer is shown a picture of the product for evaluation. The third type is the prototype, which represents a working version of the product that the customer can experience directly and evaluate accordingly. The fourth type is virtual reality where the customer experiences a prototype of the product via computer simulation.

With each of these concept tests, a different response is pulled out of the customer. Thus, one may use each concept test individually and then aggregate responses from each test to get a more robust understanding of the customer and customer perceptions. For example, one might begin with showing the customer a series of narrative product statements and ask for an initial reaction. The use of an initial narrative concept test will pull out a gestalt view of whether the idea is valid. The customer can then be shown a series of pictures alongside the narrative product statements and query feedback. The use of pictures with the narrative will address whether the proposed form is valid in the eyes of the customer. Next, the customer can be offered the opportunity to directly experience the product via a prototype or computer simulation. Concluding with the prototype or virtual reality test will assess whether the customer experience as proposed is valid and within the expectations of customers.

Questions to be asked during each of these concept tests can vary, but a critical question concerns likelihood of purchase. Other questions should gauge customers' preferences toward possible product attributes, price, and purchase location.

Lead User Analysis

A technique that can be employed during concept testing is lead user analysis (see von Hippel 1988). As suggested by the name, the technique focuses on those customers designated as "lead users" who reflect needs and wants of the main market early on, possibly several years before these needs and wants emerge in the bulk of the marketplace. Lead users, who are typically the first 3.5 percent of the market that buy a new product, reflect these needs and wants because they are positioned to benefit significantly by obtaining a solution to those needs. The premise is that if one can tap into lead users and identify their needs and wants, then such foresight can be incorporated into the development of products aimed at the mainstream market.

The lead user methodology begins with specification of the product market segment. Failure to hone in on a well-defined segment could lead to an imprecise focus on needs and wants or a focus on the wrong needs and wants, and so this first step is critical and requires keen attention (this is the crux and difficulty of lead user analysis). Once the product market segment is identified, trends in the segment and lead users affected by these trends are identified. These lead users are then canvassed and observed to develop new product specifications. The last step is to test these specifications and related product concepts stemming from them with routine, main market users.

Lead user analysis is not necessarily easy to apply, and many companies have found it difficult to identify proper lead users. Assuming one can identify lead users, Geoffrey Moore (1995) points out in his book *Crossing the Chasm* that lead users sometimes do not reflect the same concerns as the main market, and can be misleading in terms of what a market will truly accept. Lead user analysis can be a powerful attribute forecasting technique but careful application and interpretation of results are strongly recommended.

Product Use Testing

The second type of testing is product use testing. This type of testing serves to evaluate the functionality of the product offering and address the question of whether the product under consideration reflects the proper technical attributes to deliver the functionality expected (in other words, does the product work?).

Product testing can be three types. Alpha and beta testing are the two predominant forms of product testing, while gamma testing is the third type of product testing. Alpha testing relies on company employees as surrogate representatives of customers to evaluate product functionality. Alpha testing is conducted internally to the company in order to prevent the idea from prematurely entering the public domain and ensure that the product functions properly before involving parties outside the company. Beta and gamma testing rely on customers to evaluate the product, and thus, testing is done outside of the company. Customers can include key experts, lead users, and opinion leaders. Beta testing is shorter in term than gamma testing, and is commonplace in the software industry due to the common reliance on offering beta versions of software for customers to evaluate. Gamma testing is longer term in nature and is primarily used in the pharmaceutical industry to evaluate the efficacy and possible side effects of new drug formulations.

Market Testing

The third type of customer testing is market testing. Market testing serves to evaluate the appropriateness and customer acceptance of the proposed marketing plan and answer the question of whether the proposed marketing strategy will work as planned. Three general categories of market testing exist, with each category containing a distinct set of techniques.

The first category of market testing is called pseudo sale. The pseudo-sale category includes the two techniques of speculative selling and premarket testing. The former is usually used in business-to-business settings where a salesperson will make a pitch about a new product not yet for sale. Premarket testing is used in consumer markets through the use of advertising testing and other promotion testing. Mock-ups of these promotional materials are shown to customers for their opinion and reaction to the product, often through the use of mall intercepts and Web panels. Consulting companies like BASES and M/A/R/C Research are premarket testing companies.

The second category of market testing is called controlled sales and includes three types of techniques: informal selling, direct marketing, and minimarkets. Informal selling is typically performed at trade shows, where salespeople can show the product, informally approach customers, make the pitch, and see if the customer will actually buy the product. Direct marketing involves focused selling efforts on a particular market segment or target market, which receives information about the product and is offered the opportunity to purchase it. Some catalog shopping companies may add a new product to a special catalog that is sent only to a particular segment/target market to gauge the market response that this new product will generate. Minimarkets entail selling the product in only certain stores within a specific geographic location, fully supported by promotional materials expected to be used when the product is fully launched. General Mills used a minimarket to test market demand for Yoplait Custard-Style Yogurt by placing the product in only a few select stores around the Minneapolis area, along with expected grocery store promotional materials. Results encouraged the decision to move forward with a national launch (Quelch and Teopaco 1986).

The third category of market testing is called full-scale and represents the actual selling of the product in a more expansive market setting than that in a controlled sales market test (normally, full-scale market tests cover a geographic region). One of the two full-scale techniques, test marketing is an extensive initiative where a representative segment of the market receives the total marketing program. Test marketing can provide an abundant supply of market information and can verify·production capacities. Several drawbacks to test marketing are its high expense, the fact that competitors can interfere with test marketing results by introducing new promotions or pricing strategies, and the risk that the test market city will not reflect the behavior of the overall market. The second full-scale technique is rollout, which represents actual launching of the product. A rollout is when a subset of the intended target market receives the product and then the company systematically introduces the new product to other parts of the target market until the entire market is covered. Many companies that use rollouts do so as a strategy to prime production capabilities, with the new product going to the smallest region first and then entering other larger regions as production capabilities improve. In this manner, production supply is balanced with market demand. While attractive, rollouts have drawbacks too: full production capabilities still must be ready even when starting with a smaller-size market, channel member acceptance and shelf-space is critical to market acceptance, competitors may be afforded time to counter the product when launched in subsequent markets, and rollouts tend to not get media attention compared to the media attention that a national launch typically receives.

Like concept testing, multiple techniques across the three categories of market testing may be employed simultaneously or in tandem. The key in using each of the techniques is to carefully examine the market testing results, determine if refinements or revisions are necessary, and then effect such changes. A fruitful role of market testing is to verify and validate forecast assumptions, and signal whether the product and its corresponding marketing plan are market acceptable and market ready.

Conjoint Analysis

One focus of customer research is to forecast customer preferences for a product's existing or potential attributes. A popular technique for doing this is called conjoint analysis, which quantitatively calculates a metric of desirability (utility) for each attribute of a given product based on customer feedback. Combinations of various attributes sum up to different total desirability scores, and depending on the combinations may include less-desirable attributes coupled with desirable attributes due to trade-offs when the customers compare attributes. This is why conjoint analysis is also referred to as trade-off analysis.

Conjoint analysis begins by establishing sets of attributes, which are used to create complete product offerings based on the combinations of these attributes. Customers then evaluate each of these product offerings. Evaluation data are collected and analyzed to calculate desirability scores of individual attributes and relative importance for each distinct set of attributes.

For example, zoom, pixels, and water resistance capability represent sets of attributes or dimensions for a digital camera. Each dimension is broken into distinct options or levels. Zoom includes the three levels of 2X, 5X, or 10X; pixels include the two levels of 2 million (MM) or 5 million; and water resistance capability includes the two levels of waterproof or water resistant. Individual levels across the three dimensions are combined procedurally to list twelve distinct product offerings (3 levels × 2 levels × 2 levels = 12 possible product offering combinations). These twelve product offerings are shown to customers who are asked to evaluate each one. Note that different ways to evaluate product offerings exist (see American Marketing Association 2000).

One simple evaluation methodology is to have customers rank the product combinations from 1 (most preferred combination) to 12 (least preferred combination). But while rankings are relatively simple to establish from the customers' viewpoint, rankings data should be converted to a "desirability" score by flipping around the rankings in order that the most preferred combination reflects that highest desirability score (in other words, higher scores mean higher desirability). With twelve combinations, rankings are converted by subtracting the ranking from thirteen (12 + 1). Average desirability scores of each level are now calculated by averaging the desirability scores of all combinations containing the respective level.

Consider Customer 1 provides the data shown in Table 4.1, which is converted to desirability scores. Average desirability scores can be calculated for each individual level per dimension by averaging the desirability scores for combinations including that particular level. For example, the average desirability for 2X Zoom is 4.5, which is the aver-

Table 4.1

Customer Conjoint Analysis Data

Dimensions				
Zoom	Pixels	Water resistance	Customer provided rankings of combinations	Desirability scores
5X	2MM	WR	10	3
10X	2MM	WR	8	5
2X	2MM	WR	12	1
5X	2MM	WP	9	4
10X	2MM	WP	7	6
2X	2MM	WP	11	2
5X	5MM	WR	4	9
10X	5MM	WR	2	11
2X	5MM	WR	6	7
5X	5MM	WP	3	10
10X	5MM	WP	1	12
2X	5MM	WP	5	8

age of all product combinations that contain the 2X level [((1 + 2 + 7 + 8)/4) = 4.5]; the average desirability for the 5X Zoom is 6.5, which is the average of all product combinations containing the 5X level [((3 + 4 + 9 + 10)/4) = 6.5]; and the average desirability for 10X Zoom is 8.5, which is the average of all product combinations containing the 10X level [((5 + 6 + 11 + 12)/4) = 8.5]. Based on these calculations, this customer finds 10X more desirable than 5X and much more desirable than 2X; one could interpret the results as suggesting that 10X is almost two times more desirable that 2X. Similar calculations can be made to determine the average desirability for the remaining levels (refer to Table 4.1): 2 MM Pixels with an average desirability of 3.5 versus 5 MM Pixels with an average desirability of 9.5, and water resistant with an average desirability of 6 versus waterproof with an average desirability of 7. Note that when there are only two levels the desirabilities will add up to the number of combinations plus one (in the given example, the two levels should add up to thirteen).

Two types of analyses can now proceed after the average desirabilities have been calculated. One analysis compares the summed or total desirability scores across all possible attribute-level combinations. That is, the average desirability scores for each level associated with a given combination are added together to provide a summed desirability score. For example, the summed desirability for the 5X, 5MM, and WR combination is 22 (6.5 + 9.5 + 6 = 22). These summed desirability scores can be used to compare combinations and determine which ones are close in summed desirability. This is beneficial when there is a need to substitute one combination for another because of the inability to deliver a particular attribute level. Summed combinations also are useful in distinguishing those combinations that provide "positive" versus "negative" desirability. Positive versus negative desirability is determined by observing whether specific levels are above or below the midpoint value. Those levels above the midpoint value would represent positive desirability, and those below the midpoint value would represent negative desirability (a desirability value equivalent to the midpoint value would signify neutrality or indifference). For the given example, the midpoint value is 6.5 on each dimension. Those levels above 6.5 indicate positive desirability, so those levels reflecting much higher values than 6.5 are considered more desirable. The levels of 10X, 5MM, and waterproof provide positive desirability in the eyes of customer one; the combination of these levels would represent the highest level of desirability (8.5 + 9.5 + 7 = 25). Providing these three levels may not always be feasible, though, so other feasible combinations need to be identified. Those items above the summed midpoint would suggest desirable combinations—combinations that the customer would find still desirable. The summed midpoint is calculated by multiplying the midpoint value by the number of dimensions. In the given example, 6.5 times three dimensions calculates a summed midpoint of 19.5. Those combinations with summed desirability scores above 19.5 would be considered desirable and feasible combinations (trade-offs). As shown in Table 4.2, six combinations reflect positive desirability.

A second popular analysis involves calculating the relative importance of each dimension. This analysis begins by calculating the range of average desirability scores per each dimension. For example, the Zoom dimension reflects a range of 4, which is the difference between the high and low average desirability scores (8.5 – 4.5 = 4). The Pixels dimension has a range of 6 (9.5 – 3.5), and the Water Resistance Capability dimension has a range of 1 (7 – 6 = 1). The relative importance of each dimension is calculated by totaling these ranges and determining the proportion of the total that each dimension provides. For example, the total of the range values equals 11 (6 + 4 + 1). The relative importance of the Zoom dimension is 36 percent, calculated by 4 divided 11

Table 4.2

Conjoint Analysis Results for All Possible Combinations

Zoom	Pixels	Water resistance	Summed desirability scores	Desirability (difference from midpoint value)	Feasible/ desirable combination
5X	2MM	WR	16	–3.5	
10X	2MM	WR	18	–1.5	
2X	2MM	WR	14	–5.5	
5X	2MM	WP	17	–2.5	
10X	2MM	WP	19	–0.5	
2X	2MM	WP	15	–4.5	
5X	5MM	WR	22	2.5	Yes
10X	5MM	WR	24	4.5	Yes
2X	5MM	WR	20	0.5	Yes
5X	5MM	WP	23	3.5	Yes
10X	5MM	WP	25	5.5	Yes
2X	5MM	WP	21	1.5	Yes
Summed midpoint value		19.5			

or 36 percent. This percentage is interpreted as the Zoom dimension accounting for 36 percent of the variability associated with Customer 1's desire for the digital camera product. The Pixels dimension accounts for 55 percent (6 divided by 11) of this variability, and the Water Use dimension accounts for 9 percent (1 divided by 11) of the variability. The conclusion from the relative importance analysis is that Pixel accounts for over half of the desire that Customer 1 has in the digital camera product. Zoom accounts for one-third of the desire in the digital camera product. Therefore, most product development attention should emphasize Pixel. A loose interpretation is that Pixels has the potential to drive 55 percent of the demand and decision making behind purchases for the digital camera product.

Conjoint analysis can obviously become cumbersome when numerous attributes and multiple options per attribute are considered. The addition of one more level to the Pixel dimension would increase the number of combinations to 18 (3 × 3 × 2) combinations. The addition of a fourth dimension with two levels to the original set of data would have resulted in the need to consider 24 (3 × 2 × 2 × 2) combinations, doubling the number of combinations that the customer would need to consider and likely leading to customer fatigue during the ranking exercise. Hence, only those attributes and levels considered critical should be evaluated.

If the number of attributes and levels results in a set of combinations greater than say twelve combinations, advanced analytical approaches are available to quickly eliminate undesired product attributes (American Marketing Association 2000). These advanced approaches are statistically sophisticated in nature, although various software packages and consulting agencies are available to assist in performing conjoint analysis studies, for example, Sawtooth Software (Sequim, Washington).

A final comment is that this example used data from only one customer when typical conjoint analyses involve multiple customers. Various methodologies for merging multiple customer data exist, with the simplest approach being the averaging of results across individual customers' rank data. For further reading on conjoint analysis, see Dolan (1990), Hair et al. (1998), and American Marketing Association (2000).

Quality Function Deployment

Developed in the 1960s for use in Japan's Kobe shipyards, later adopted by the Japanese and U.S. automobile industries, and subsequently adopted by other industries, quality function deployment (QFD) is a methodology that purposely links customer needs with technical specifications in an attempt to create an "optimal" product configuration. Whereas conjoint analysis looks at the combination of attributes and the trade-offs that customers may make in deciding on the product to purchase, QFD evaluates the attributes distinct from each other. And though different in approach, recent work shows how QFD can be used in conjunction with conjoint analysis (see Pullman, Moore, and Wardell 2002).

The original QFD methodology comprises four stages of evaluation, beginning at a top level with the linkage between customer benefits sought and product specifications. The next three levels detail product specifications down to the level of parts specifications and further down to the level of manufacturing process specifications (see Figure 4.1). In most cases, companies have found that managing the QFD process across these four stages is extremely complex and time-consuming. Most companies therefore find the most expeditious approach is to focus on the top level of evaluation, which links customer benefits sought to product specifications (technical specifications). This level is commonly referred to as the "House of Quality" (Hauser and Clausing 1988).

The House of Quality illustrates the relationships between the voice of the customer (VOC) and the voice of the engineer (VOE), where the

Figure 4.1 **The Four Levels of Quality Function Deployment (QFD)**

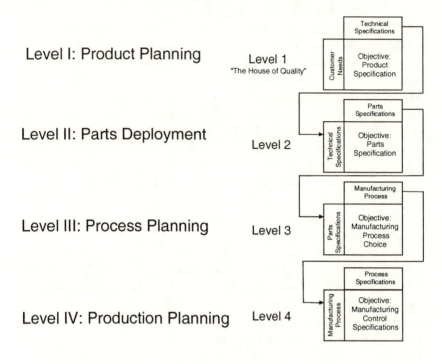

VOC emphasizes what the customer wants to get out of using the product or product benefits and the VOE delineates the technical characteristics of the product. This is accomplished via a matrix approach where the VOC is located on the rows of the matrix showing customer needs and the VOE is located in the columns of the matrix showing engineering parameters (see Figure 4.2). For example, a customer describing a pencil may state a need for it not to easily roll when placed on a hard surface, whereas an engineer may describe a similar consideration as pencil hexagonality (a typical customer would not use the terminology of hexagonality). The matrix indicates a strong relationship between these two issues, and so hexagonality should be a design consideration if reducing the propensity of the pencil to roll becomes a priority.

Voice of the customer information is collected through VOC studies. These studies collect three important pieces of information: (1) customer needs/benefits sought, (2) importance of each of these needs/benefits relative to each other, and (3) evaluations of the company's and

Figure 4.2 **QFD: The House of Quality**

A - 1 Pencil	length	time between sharpening	lead dust generated	hexagonality		rate of importance	company now	competitor x	competitor y	plan	ratio of improvement	sales points	absolute wt.	demanded wt.
Easy to hold	42			42		3	4	3	3	4	1	1	3.0	14%
Does not smear		69	207			4	5	4	5	5	1	1.2	4.8	23%
Point lasts	44	396	132			5	4	5	3	5	1.25	1.5	9.4	44%
Does not roll	19			171		3	3	3	3	4	1.333	1	4.0	19%
Total	105	465	339	213	1122						Total		21.2	100%
%	9%	41%	30%	19%	100%									
company now	5"	3pgs	3g	70%										
competitor x	5"	5pgs	2g	80%										
competitor y	4"	2.5pgs	4g	60%										
plan	5.5"	6pgs	2g	80%										

Main Correlations

◎ 9 = strong correlation

○ 3 = some correlation

△ 1 = possible correlation

Sales Points = 1.5, 1.2, or 1

competitors' current offerings in satisfying these needs/benefits. For many companies, this information is robust enough, and so many companies choose not to perform a full QFD analysis, instead focusing on analyses of the ample data collected during a VOC study to clarify what specific needs/benefits customers have. This information is then used to frame the product's technical specifications.

Other companies take the next step with VOC data and attempt to match it with technical data, the VOE, in accordance with the QFD methodology. The VOE data represent specific technical characteristics (technical specifications) of the product. Such characteristics may derive from the product protocol or correspond to those characteristics that can be readily tested. In addition to specifying technical characteristics, VOE data will indicate a desired course of action for each respective characteristic in terms of reducing or increasing the magnitude of this characteristic. For example, the engineering team for a new car in specifying the technical characteristic of weight may indicate a desire to reduce weight. The third element of VOE data is specifying the relationships between each of the technical characteristics, that is, how would reducing the car weight impact wind resistance? These relationships are specified in the matrix above the technical characteristics called the "trade-off roof." Both negative and positive correlations between the technical specifications would be indicated. A fourth possible element that may be included in VOE data is the benchmark data comparing the focal company product with those of competitors on the given technical characteristics. Benchmark data would assist in determining quantitative targets for each of the given technical characteristics.

As shown in Figure 4.2, four customer needs (VOC data) are articulated: easy to hold, does not smear, point lasts, and does not roll. Each of these needs are rated on their importance on a 1- to 5-point scale, where 1 is "not important" and 5 is "very important" in the column following the technical specifications. The needs are also evaluated across the company's and its top competitors' products using a 1- to 5-point scale, where 1 is "very weak on this need" and 5 is "very strong on this need." As shown, "point lasts" is the most important need (rate of importance = 5); the company is evaluated as below competitor X on this need and above competitor Y. The column after the competitor evaluation data is the "Plan," which represents what the company wants customers to perceive. The plan therefore represents a management expectation to be set. The next column, ratio of improvement, is the calculation of plan divided by the company now. Given that the company scored a 4 on "point lasts," it has a plan of 5, which calculates a 1.25 ratio of improvement (5 divided by 4). This can be interpreted as meaning that the company wants to improve market perceptions of "point lasts" by 25 percent (a ratio of 1 would represent 0 percent or no change). Sales points are incremental bumps to particular needs if management or the sales force believes that the respective need is necessary for creating a competitive advantage. In the given example, three sales points are possible: a score of 1 (no bump), a score of 1.2 (slight bump), or a score of 1 5 (bump). Absolute weight is calculated by multiplying the rate of importance by the ratio of improvement by the sales points. "Point lasts" has an absolute weight of 9.4 (5 × 1.25 × 1.5). Demanded weight is the relative percentage of the absolute weight to the total absolute weight. In the example, the total absolute weight is 21.2 (the sum of the absolute weights for easy to hold, does not smear, point lasts, and does not roll). The demanded weight for point lasts is .44 or 44 percent, calculated by dividing 9.4 by 21.2. The use of demanded weight allows for the interpretation that 44 percent of product demand is based on the point lasting. Those items with the highest percentages should be prioritized during engineering and technical development activities. Note that some QFD methodologies prefer not to use sales points because of the contention that only customers should dictate how needs should be weighted. The sales point system is presented because it may be useful in highlighting emerging needs during one's application of the Kano Model, which will be discussed later in this chapter.

Following the prioritizing of customer needs, the relationships between each of the customer needs and technical characteristics are examined. In most cases, an intense discussion is held between marketing and engineering personnel to clarify these relationships. This highlights the key benefit of QFD as a tool for facilitating interdepartmental communication. Assuming that consensus is reached, which may take time, the correlations between the respective needs and characteristics are listed. In the given example, three types of correlations can be listed: a weak correlation, which is given the weight of 1; some correlation, which is given the weight of a 3; and a strong correlation, which is given the weight of a 9. Using these weights, the relationships between each customer and technical specification are weighted by multiplying the weight of the relationship by the demanded weight for the respective customer need. For example, the relationship between "point lasts" and "time between sharpenings" is indicated to be a strong correlation, which is a weight of 9. Multiplying this weight by "point lasts" demand weight of 44 percent equals a score of 396. Completing the calculations across all cells and then totaling the columns provides a total score for each technical specification. Taking the relative percentage of each column to the total score suggests how much of demand is predicated on the respective technical characteristic. For example, "time between sharpenings" has a score of 465, which represents 41 percent of the total score. This can be loosely interpreted as suggesting that 44 percent of product demand is predicated on addressing the "time between sharpening" characteristic. Now engineering has a priority list of which technical characteristics to focus on during technical development. The respective engineering benchmarks serve as targets to drive the technical development process.

The Kano Model

The Kano model is a framework that can supplement decisions in the QFD analysis. Specifically, the Kano model attempts to push product development activities from satisfying customers to delighting customers.

Proposed by Dr. Noriaki Kano in the 1980s, the Kano model suggests that there are three types of product attributes or features that can be designed into a product: assumed features, expected features, and delighting features. Assumed features are basic product attributes that customers equate to the particular product; assumed features do not drive customer satisfaction, but rather, minimize customer dissatisfaction. As more and more assumed features are designed into the product, a potential customer will be less and less dissatisfied but never satisfied. For example, an assumed feature of an automobile roadside assistance service club (e.g., American Automobile Association) would be the service club answering the telephone and sending out a tow truck for roadside assistance when the customer called for one due to a flat tire. This is a basic service that members pay for and assume to be a standard feature.

Expected features are product attributes that by nature of their name are expected in the product. The distinction of expected features is that they have a linear relationship with customer satisfaction in that if the expected features are better than customers' expectations, customers will be satisfied. Expected features are therefore referred to as "linear satisfiers," and often correspond to service time. For example, the sooner the tow truck arrives on the scene, the more satisfied the auto service club customer will be.

Delighting features are unexpected product attributes that surpass customer expectations of the product or service. Unexpected product attributes must be perceived as adding value to the product and not just represent superfluous product attributes. Naturally, the customer having a flat tire would expect the tire to be repaired or the car towed for repair. If the tow truck personnel not only fixed the flat tire, but in the same amount of time, washed the car and changed the oil at no extra charge, the customer would most likely be very delighted.

The relationship between the three features and customer satisfaction is illustrated in Figure 4.3. The objective is to carefully plan assumed features, expected features, and delighting features into a product to balance product cost with customer satisfaction, hopefully maximizing satisfaction while minimizing cost.

The Kano model can be linked to the QFD methodology via the sales points application. Specifically, the weights of 1, 1.2, and 1.5 can be used

Figure 4.3 **The Kano Model**

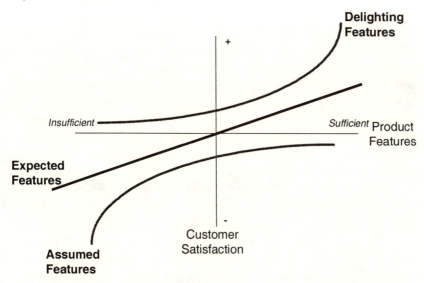

to represent assumed, expected, and delighting features, respectively, which would be determined through customer interviews, managerial judgment, and company experience. However, one must realize that features identified as delighting in a current version of a product or service often become expected features in the next version. Thus, only a few delighting features should be used in each product design, otherwise customers will expect or even assume these features in future product versions. It is also possible that building too many delighting features into the product may make it too pricey for customers to afford or cost-prohibitive for the company to produce. Stein and Iansiti (1995) offer a methodology for operationalizing the Kano Model. This methodology involves asking two questions for each feature, one positive in nature and the other negative, and having respondents indicate whether they like, must have, are neutral, can live with, or dislike that feature. Features are then typed as "delighter," "linear satisfier," "must be/must have," "indifferent quality element," "reverse quality element," or "questionable," in accordance with Table 4.3.

Key Concepts

Concept Testing
Lead User Analysis
Product Use Testing
Market Testing

Table 4.3

Operationalizing the Kano Model

Result of positive question	Result of negative question				
	Like	Must be	Neutral	Live with	Dislike
Like	Q	D	D	D	L
Must be	R	I	I	I	M
Neutral	R	I	I	I	M
Live with	R	I	I	I	M
Dislike	R	R	R	R	Q

Source: Adapted from "Understanding Customer Needs" by Ellen Stein and Marco Iansiti, HBS Case Note # 9–695–051, 1995.

Notes:

D = Delighter
. . . the delighter is not expected so its absence does not cause dissatisfaction. If the need is met, however, it will increase satisfaction

L = Linear Satisfier
. . . the better the product is at meting the need, the better the customer likes it.

M = Must Be/Must Have
. . . no matter how well the product meets the need, the customer simply accepts it as something that is expected. However, if the need is not met, the customer is very dissatisfied.

I = Indifferent Quality Element
. . . produces neither satisfaction nor dissatisfaction in the customer, regardless of whether it is met in the product.

R = Reverse Quality Element
. . . creates dissatisfaction when fulfilled or satisfaction when not fulfilled. This implies that either the survey question was not written correctly, or that the trait is undesirable to the customer.

Q = Questionable Result
. . . the relationship does not make sense and should be investigated to determine whether the survey question was not written correctly or something unique is occurring.

Conjoint Analysis
Quality Function Deployment
Kano Model

Discussion Questions

1. What is the purpose of concept testing?
2. What is the purpose of product use testing?
3. What is the purpose of market testing?
4. What insights does conjoint analysis provide?
5. What is quality function deployment?

5

Time Series Techniques for
New Product Forecasting

When sales data are available, several options exist for applying "quantitative" analyses. These quantitative analyses mostly fall into the two general categories of time series analysis and regression analyses. The present chapter discusses the use of time series analyses within the context of new product forecasting. The next chapter, chapter 6, discusses options for using regression analysis within the new product forecasting context.

Variations of time series analyses exist, depending on factors of data availability, level of analysis, and forecasting objective. For instance, cost reductions or product improvements already have preexisting sales data. These data may be used to project the impact of the new product if previous reductions or improvements had been implemented with the respective product. If no prior cost reductions or product improvements had been made, surrogate sales data may be used to develop an analogous model for predicting the sales bump due to the cost reduction or product improvement. The critical assumption when using an analogous model is whether the respective product is akin to the surrogate product. Many companies often accept this assumption, making analogous or "looks-like" forecasting models a particularly popular approach with line extensions where prior line extensions are used to project new line extensions within the same product line.

Looks-like analysis may be used across a number of new product forecasting cases such as new use, new market, new category entry, and new-to-the-world products. In the case of new-to-the-world products, a more advanced analogous modeling approach called diffusion modeling can be employed. While not really a looks-like approach in the truest sense, diffusion modeling attempts to portray the life-cycle pattern of a technological innovation based on assumptions of given parameters and market behavior knowledge. Each of these time series approaches is now discussed.

Looks-Like Analysis (Analogous Forecasting)

Analogous forecasting, commonly called "looks-like" or "like" analysis, is a forecasting technique that employs historical data patterns to model a new product's sales patterns. In the case of cost reductions and product improvements, data will come from the respective product's history. In the case of line extensions, new use, new market, new category entries, and new-to-the-world products, historical data from other new products would be used.

The critical assumption of looks-like analysis is that the analogous data reflect a similar level of innovation and similar market conditions and result in applicable new product sales patterns for the new product. Because sales data patterns rarely replicate in absolute terms across products and market conditions, the use of absolute sales data is discouraged. Product offerings, however, can and do often reflect similar patterns in terms of relative sales patterns. A relative analogous modeling approach is therefore prescribed. That is, analyses should use relative data in the form of percentages such as the percent of sales in a particular month across a given time horizon. The use of percent sales per month is especially useful in creating launch profiles.

Creating Launch Profiles

Launch profiles represent a pictorial view of the new product sales trajectory in the first year. While the term "sales" is used, launch profiles can be developed to suggest the trajectory of shipments, final demand, and so on. A simple approach for constructing these profiles is to sum the demand volume for a previously launched similar product, or average first-year data across a set of previously launched products within a product line/category. First-year data would mean either twelve data points should be collected if forecasting monthly (assuming a twelve-month year, though some systems reflect thirteen four-week periods) or fifty-two data points should be collected if forecasting weekly (assuming a fifty-two-week year, though some systems reflect a fifty-three-

Table 5.1

Constructing a Looks-Like Model

Month	Product 1 first year sales	Relative percentage	Cumulative percentage
1	11,908	4	4
2	77,907	28	32
3	42,716	15	47
4	34,768	12	60
5	18,653	7	67
6	18,481	7	73
7	8,836	3	76
8	12,632	5	81
9	13,617	5	86
10	23,446	8	94
11	6,366	2	96
12	10,257	4	100

week year). Dividing each period (month or week) by the total volume would provide a percent of sales per first period, second period, third period, and so on. Each month's individual percentages represent a relative percentage (called the relative distribution model), and the running total of these relative percentages provides the cumulative percentage (called the cumulative distribution model). The relative distribution model is useful for proportioning out an annual estimate over the first year. The cumulative distribution model is useful for determining the percent of sales to occur at different points in the first year.

Use of a launch profile model only gives a likely trajectory of baseline sales, not a hard prediction of actual sales. Thus, the use of launch profiles and looks-like analysis techniques should be viewed as offering a baseline directional account for new product sales, not as a method for generating specific numeric forecasts (although the approach will suggest a numeric baseline forecast). Baseline estimates should be evaluated and, if need be, augmented through judgment and market intelligence as part of the sales and operations process (previously discussed in chapter 2).

An example of a looks-like model in the form of a launch profile is presented in Table 5.1. Using first year's sales of a former product, a looks-like model is developed to predict percent of sales per month in the first year and percent of sales distributed over the first year. Using Product 1's launch history, the annual first year forecast of 1,000,000 units for Prod-

Table 5.2

Evaluation of a Looks-Like Model

Month	Product 1 (%)	Product 2 (%)	Product 3 (%)	Average relative (%)	Cumulative (%)
1	4	15	16	12	12
2	28	2	10	13	25
3	15	7	13	11	36
4	12	15	9	12	49
5	7	15	6	9	58
6	7	6	7	6	64
7	3	7	5	5	70
8	5	8	5	6	75
9	5	7	9	7	82
10	8	10	8	9	91
11	2	4	6	4	95
12	4	5	6	5	100

uct 2 can be proportioned out as follows: 40,000 units in month 1; 280,000 units in month 2; 150,000 units in month 3; 120,000 units in month 4; 70,000 units in month 5; 70,000 units in month 6; 30,000 units in month 7; 50,000 units in month 8; 50,000 units in month 9; 80,000 units in month 10; 20,000 units in month 11; and 40,000 units in month 12.

Table 5.2 shows that the sales for Product 1 did not accurately forecast sales of Product 2 and Product 3, however, the looks-like model of Product 1 offers a directional view of product sales. Interestingly, by the sixth month, the looks-like models appear to converge. As mentioned, an average of previous product sales per month can be used to create relative percent sales and cumulative percent sales looks-like curves to predict future products.

The averaging approach is a simple way to create a set of new product launch templates or launch "meta-profiles" or "meta-curves." A more sophisticated approach is to apply curve-fitting techniques to the cumulative curve and determine which mathematical model best "fits" the data. While best fit by a linear model is possible, nonlinear curve-fitting techniques should be examined, including logarithmic, polynomial, power, S-curve, and exponential curves. Analysis using the trend line option found in Microsoft Excel or curve-fitting routines found in statistical software packages like SPSS can be used to determine which model best fits the data.

A number of curve-fitting techniques were applied to the data found in Table 5.2. The coefficient of determination (R-squared), which indi-

Table 5.3

Model Fit Using *R*-Squared Values Across Products 1, 2, and 3

Model	Product 1 (%)	Product 2 (%)	Product 3 (%)	Average *R*-squared value (%)
Linear	89.20	98.10	98.70	95.33
Logarithmic	99.60	90.50	94.20	94.77
Quadratic	96.90	98.80	99.30	98.33
Cubic	99.30	99.10	99.80	99.40
Power	82.60	95.80	99.60	92.67
S-Curve	98.80	76.20	89.60	88.20
Growth	56.00	89.50	87.40	77.63
Exponential	56.00	89.50	87.40	77.63

cates the percent of sales variation explained by the model, is used to interpret the results. The average values of R-squared values across the three products and curve-fitting models suggest that the cubic model is a representative model. In other words, the average values of R-squared suggest that the cubic model on average explains more of the variation in the given sales data versus other models (refer to Table 5.3). Naturally, as new demand data becomes available with future new products, these looks-like models would be refreshed with the new data.

Mapping Supply and Demand Launch Profiles

A variety of companies have found it useful to establish distinct profiles for both product supply and market demand across product groupings. In this way, profiles of supply and demand curves, especially covering the launch period, can be integrated properly to ascertain what levels of supply are necessary to sustain demand, and conversely, what demand events will impact supply. These models are also referred to as product push and market pull models.

The supply profile gives particular visibility to the potential for the "pipeline fill" effect. Common in the case of consumer product companies, the supply phenomenon known as pipeline fill is the loading of inventory into channel member distribution centers and retail locations. Consumer electronics companies call this the "floor set" phenomenon, where retailers are stocking product on store shelves and placing product on the retail floor for show and demonstration.

The demand profile should include visibility to consumer seasonality and promotional/holiday activity. Many consumer product companies, as well as business-to-business companies, experience distinct seasonal patterns in sales (demand). Products like swimming pool chemicals and suntan lotion will certainly experience higher demand during summer months since these are traditional summer time products. Consumer sales promotions that the company offers year after year at the same time of year or connected to a specific holiday should be considered in a launch profile too. Candy naturally will experience higher final consumer demand during the Halloween and Christmas holidays. Wide screen television sales in the United States tend to increase in December and January due in large part to college football bowls and the Super Bowl.

An example of supply and market demand launch profiles within the consumer electronics industry is presented in Figure 5.1. These profiles represent one full year of sales to provide baseline trajectories, and equate to the life cycle of a product model year (the distinction of consumer electronics and other industries like automobiles is the ability to equate a single model year to one full year of sales; product life cycles in other industries like consumer packaged goods and pharmaceuticals normally extend far beyond the first year). As shown, the model year consists of four phases: floor set, plateau, high season, and phase out. The supply profile experiences a spike in quantity in order to build retailer inventories, and diminishes, levels off, and spikes to a lesser degree at the end of the model year, and then tapers down. In contrast, the consumer demand profile builds slowly to a plateau level, eventually spiking during the high season, and then tapering off. Linking these two models can help to determine proper channel inventories and production plans across the year. These profiles also can be altered to account for sales promotions, price changes, new retailer partners, and so on, and assist in the derivation of the new product forecast.

Diffusion Modeling

Diffusion models are powerful time series approaches. Similar to looks-like analyses, these models attempt to fit the sales trajectory of new technologies, typically reflecting an "S" shape and fittingly called S-curve models (see Figure 5.2). The keen distinction of these models is their statistical sophistication coupled with advanced modeling capabilities. In essence, diffusion models provide a mathematical model to

Figure 5.1   **Launch Profile Methodology: Mapping Supply and Demand Profiles**

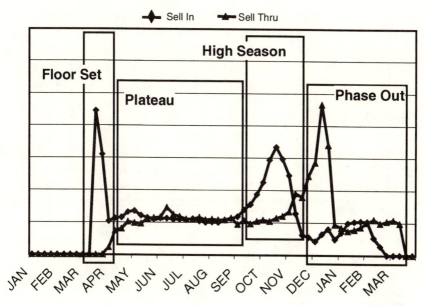

underlie the shape of the cumulative sales pattern, and analogous launch patterns can be used in conjunction with diffusion modeling. Diffusion models therefore can take many forms. Readers are referred to Mahajan and Peterson (1985), Mahajan and Wind (1986), Mahajan, Muller, and Bass (1990), Lilien and Rangaswamy (1998), and Lilien, Rangaswamy, and Van den Bulte (1999), all of whom provide more detailed discussions of diffusion models.

The most popular diffusion model is the Bass model, which is predicated on two components: the mass media effect, also referred to as the coefficient of innovation, and the word of mouth effect, also referred to as the coefficient of imitation. These two components are represented mathematically by way of the following formula:

$$n(t) = p[m - N(t)] + q\left(\frac{N(t)}{m}\right)[m - N(t)]$$

$n(t) = [\,p \times \text{Remaining Potential}] + [\,q \times \text{Adopters} \times \text{Remaining Potential}]$

Innovation Effect   *Imitation Effect*

Figure 5.2 **The S-Curve Model**

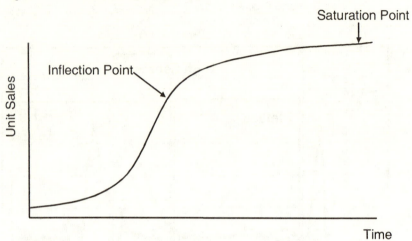

where

m = the potential number of adopters (adopters = sales);

$n(t)$ = the number of adopters at time t;

$N(t)$ = the cumulative number of adopters at time t;

p = coefficient of innovation;

q = coefficient of imitation.

An example of the Bass diffusion model is shown in Figure 5.3. Based on analogous products, p equals .10 and q equals .25. Management proposes a seven-year product life with a maximum sales level of 1,000,000 units (m = 1,000,000). Based on the Bass model, Year 1 would incur sales of 100,000 due to only an innovation effect. The annual forecast would be calculated as follows:

$$\text{Year 1 Forecast} = (.1 \times [1,000,000 - 0]) + (.25 \times [0/1,000,000] \times [1,000,000 - 0] = 100,000 + 0 = 100,000$$

The forecast for Year 2 would consist of sales from both innovation and imitation effects as shown below:

$$\text{Year 2 Forecast} = (.1 \times [1,000,000 - 100,000]) + (.25 \times [100,000/1,000,000] \times [1,000,000 - 100,000] = 90,000 + 91,000 = 181,000$$

Figure 5.3 **The Bass Model**

p	0.1	q	0.25	m	1,000,000

Year	N(t)	Innovation Effect	Imitation Effect	Forecast	Cumulative Forecast
One	0	100,000	0	100,000	100,000
Two	100,000	90,000	91,000	181,000	281,000
Three	281,000	71,900	92,810	164,710	445,710
Four	445,710	55,429	94,457	149,886	595,596
Five	595,596	40,440	95,956	136,396	731,992
Six	731,992	26,801	97,320	124,121	856,113
Seven	856,113	14,389	98,561	112,950	969,063

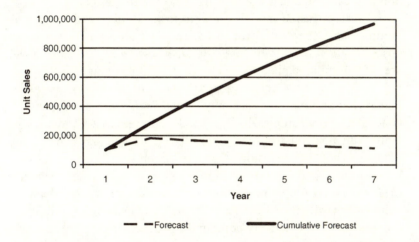

The total sales volume forecast for Years 1 and 2 (cumulative sales through Year 2) equals 100,000 + 181,000 = 281,000 units. Forecast data for all years are provided in Figure 5.3.

To successful apply the Bass model, the analyst must first establish the coefficient of innovation and the coefficient of imitation. Use of analogous products is one approach for doing this by selecting values for p and q from previous, similar products. Work by Lilien, Rangaswamy, and Van den Bulte (1999) also provides results of p and q coefficients across a number of product categories.

To help in determining which products to analogously model, Thomas (1985) indicates that five bases of similarities should be considered when selecting an analogous product on which to base diffusion model components: environmental context (e.g., socioeconomic environment, regulatory environment); market structure (e.g., barriers to entry, number of competitors); buyer behavior (e.g., buyer situation, choice attributes); marketing mix strategies of the firm (e.g., promotion, pricing); and characteristics of the innovation (e.g., relative advantage over existing products, product complexity). Also, work by Choffray and Lilien (1986), Sultan, Farley, and Lehmann (1990), and Lenk and Rao (1990) provide formal procedures to incorporate data from analogous products into parameter estimation, including use of a weighted average approach for p and q values. In addition, Morrison (1999) suggests how an analyst can calculate a p and q variable from previous empirical data comprising five or more periods.

Because diffusion models are akin to looks-like models, they are predominantly beneficial for visualizing the trajectory of sales, not absolute sales. Moreover, forecasts emerging from diffusion models are often used to explain the nature of diffusion versus sales forecasting. It is also important to recognize that diffusion models rely on underlying assumptions that may or may not represent full market conditions. For example, the Bass model assumes that: (1) market potential remains constant over time, (2) market potential will be eventually reached, (3) diffusion of an innovation is independent of other innovations, (4) the nature of innovation does not change over time, (5) there are no supply restrictions, (6) product and market characteristics do not influence diffusion patterns, and (7) the market inflection point occurs at the halfway point in the products life. If one or several of these assumptions do not properly apply, other models such as the logistic and Gompertz curve might be considered. Variations of the Bass model and other diffusion models have also been developed to overcome the potential limitations posed by the assumptions of the Bass model, such as addressing pent-up demand (preselling issues); marketing plan differences across new products; relaxed assumptions about life-cycle curve symmetry; and changes in market conditions, including competitive response.

To help guide managers, Lilien, Rangaswamy, and Van den Bulte (1999) make the following observations about the Bass model and diffusion models in general along with prescriptions for their application:

- Diffusion models are often best left in the hands of analysts and modelers; managers should serve in the role of defining the issues, engage in the diffusion model development process, and get quick access to model results (see Kalish 1985).

- Diffusion models can provide a disciplined approach to support product launch timing decision (a situation where there is clearly no available sales data) where product quality is assumed to vary over time (see Kalish and Lilien 1986).
- A formal approach to selecting analogous p and q parameters can help improve the acceptance of a diffusion model (see Choffray and Lilien 1986).
- The diffusion modeling process itself can provide key management benefits, such as identification of necessary data and refinement of managerial judgment that are critical diffusion model inputs (see Bayus 1987).
- Laboratory-based data can be used as inputs to diffusion models, producing prelaunch positioning and long-term product planning implications (see Urban and Hauser 1993).
- With sufficient care and blending of survey data, judgments, and some sales data, diffusion models can provide a systematic approach to address a wide range of new product planning challenges; sample selection and survey question design is critical in developing valid, supportable results (see Sawhney and Eliashberg 1996; Lattin and Roberts 1998; Mahajan, Muller, and Wind 2000).

Composite Curve Approach

An emerging time series approach for new product forecasting is the composite curve approach. This approach takes the output of various analyses previously discussed, including looks-like curves for market demand, looks-like curves for pipeline fill, diffusion curves for market penetration, and so on, and merges them into a composite forecast. Coupled with indexes for relevant factors like customer sensitivity to price, advertising, and special promotions, a baseline sales figure is augmented. In essence, the composite curve approach serves as an analytical representation for mapping a new product's supply and demand profiles. Figure 5.4 portrays the technique pictorially.

Table 5.4 illustrates a numeric example of the composite curve approach. Five factors are listed: the penetration rate (sell-through effect), the pipeline fill effect (sell-in effect), a promotion effect, a pricing policy effect, and seasonal indices. Merging these factors analytically via indexes, the expected total annual demand is decomposed across the twelve months to derive a raw shipment forecast. The raw shipment forecast is

Figure 5.4 **Composite Curve Approach**

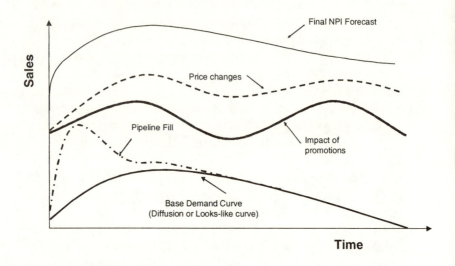

adjusted accordingly so that it meets the expected 300,000 annual total designated by management. It is imperative that discussions occur to decide whether the sales discrepancy between the raw and adjusted shipment forecasts is attainable.

Key Concepts

Looks-Like Analysis
Launch Profiles
Diffusion Modeling
Bass Model
Composite Curve Approach

Discussion Questions

1. When is it appropriate to employ looks-like analysis?
2. How can launch profiles be developed?
3. What is diffusion modeling?
4. What two components make up the Bass model?
5. What is the purpose of the composite curve approach?

Table 5.4

Numeric Example of the Composite Curve Approach

													Total
Expected total annual demand	300,000												
Adjusted shipment forecast	28,731	28,282	19,257	54,408	32,322	25,711	15,426	13,884	15,426	20,177	21,646	24,731	300,000
Raw shipment forecast	25,344	24,948	16,987	47,995	28,512	22,680	13,608	12,247	13,608	17,798	19,094	21,816	264,639
Model components													
Penetration rate (sell-through effect)	0.04	0.06	0.07	0.08	0.08	0.09	0.09	0.09	0.10	0.10	0.10	0.10	
Pipeline fill (sell-in effect)	2.40	1.80	1.08	1.80	1.08	0.84	0.60	0.48	0.48	0.48	0.48	0.48	
Promotion effect	1.10	1.10	1.08	1.01	1.00	1.00	1.00	1.00	1.00	1.03	1.02	1.01	
Pricing policy effect	1.00	1.00	1.00	1.00	1.00	1.05	1.05	1.05	1.00	1.00	1.00	1.00	
Seasonal indices	0.8	0.7	0.7	1.1	1.1	0.8	0.9	0.9	1.2	1.3	1.5		

6

Regression Analysis for
New Product Forecasting

Regression analysis examines the relationship between two or more variables and derives a representative equation expressing the relationship between these variables. One of the variables is called the dependent variable because it is "dependent" or a consequence of the other variables in the equation. These other variables are called independent variables because each of the independent variables is considered a uniquely distinct dataset. In most cases, sales will represent the dependent variable whether corresponding to shipments, orders, or point-of-sale demand, for instance. Independent variables can be a variety of possible factors, with external factors (nonsales data) often used such as specific marketing promotions, price information, and calendar holidays. Components of the sales data also may be used in various ways to forecast future sales data via an analysis called time series regression. The focus of the present chapter is the use of external variables to predict new product sales and new product sales behavior. One particular technique to be discussed is the use of dummy variables as independent variables (external factors) to represent new product policy decisions. This latter technique is indicative of an event modeling technique.

Correlation

Before beginning with regression analyses, it is useful to discuss correlation because correlation is the basis on which regression analyses are predicated. Correlation, designated by the letter "r" and the Greek symbol rho, is a metric that assesses the linear relationship between two variables. The range for correlation is between -1 and 1, with -1 representing a perfect negative relationship, 0 representing no relationship, and 1 representing a perfect positive relationship. While the numeric value of a correlation suggests strength of the linear relationship, it is best used to determine the directional nature of the linear relationship between two variables. Strength of the relationship is better determined by squaring the correlation value to calculate R-squared (or R^2). Called the coefficient of determination, R^2 is interpreted as the amount of variance explained by the linear relationship. For example, a correlation (r) of $-.3$ suggests a negative correlation between two respective variables. Squaring this value gives an R-squared value of $.09$ and suggests that the relationship explains 9 percent of the relationship between the two respective variables.

A variety of benchmarks has been offered for what represents a "significant" correlation. Mason and Lind (1996) indicate that a correlation of below $-.50$ and above $.50$ are moderate in strength. The overriding issue is how much comfort the analyst has in the amount of variance explained. Some analysts accept correlations of greater than $.3$ (or less than $-.30$) because roughly 10 percent or more of relationship between the two variables is being explained.

Regression Analyses

Regression analyses can come in many forms, including linear and non-linear regression. Discussion begins with simple linear regression followed by multiple linear regression. It then progresses to the more advanced regression analyses topics of nonlinear regression, preference regression, and logistic regression.

Simple Linear Regression

Simple linear regression analysis is the derivation of an equation between two variables. As the name suggests, simple linear regression analysis develops an equation to express the linear effect of the independent variable on the dependent variable, and thus, it is assumed that the relationship between these two variables is indeed linear in nature. If a positive relationship exists, linear means that as the independent variable increases, the dependent variable will increase by the value of the coefficient for the independent variable; if a negative relationship exists, linear means that as the independent variable increases, the dependent variable will decrease by the value of the coefficient for the independent variable.

The general equation of a simple linear regression model is as follows: $y = a + bx$, where y is the dependent variable, a is the y-intercept constant (scale constant), b is the slope, and x is the independent variable. While various methodologies can be used to construct the regression equation, the most common approach is least squares estimation, which "fits" a straight line through the data and determines an equation by minimizing the sum of squares of the vertical distances between the actual dependent variable values (actual sales) and the predicted values of the dependent variable (predicated sales using the equation).

Consider the following simple linear regression equation between the dependent variable of sales and the independent variable of price:

New Product Sales in units = 100 − 4 (price in U.S. dollars)

This equation indicates a negative relationship between sales and price, which means that when price goes up, sales go down. Using the equation, a forthcoming new product price of $5 will generate a unit sales volume of 80 units [100 − (4 x 5) = 80]. What-if analyses can be conducted subsequently to determine what the price should be to meet company expectations.

The ability of regression to evaluate various new product policies makes regression analyses a useful tool. One must be mindful when applying this equation, however. The equation suggests that if price goes to zero, then there is the opportunity to sell 100 units; conversely, if price goes to $25, then sales go to zero. Before accepting this suggestion, the analyst should evaluate the range of price that was used to develop the model. If the original input price data ranged between $4 and $6, then realistically the equation should apply only in those cases where a new price will fall within this range. Should a new price fall outside of this range, the forecaster must evaluate how applicable this equation is.

Determining the significance of the independent variable's effect on the dependent variable is based on statistical significance using the t-statistic. A t-statistic evaluates whether the independent variable contributes significantly to explaining the variation in the dependent variable. Statistical significance is often judged in terms of 95 percent confidence or a p-value of less than .05 for a two-sided test of the t-statistic. The reason for a two-sided test is because the t-statistic can be both positive and negative, where a positive value corresponds to a positive relationship and a negative value corresponds to a negative relationship. Roughly speaking, statistical significance of 95 percent confidence (p-value of less than .05) is shown when the t-statistic is above 2 or below -2.

Simple Linear Regression Using Dummy Variables

Simple linear regression can be useful in examining cost reduction and product improvement types of new products. Specifically, analysis can be performed to discern the sales bump effect of a previously enacted new product policy or event, such as a new pricing policy, a new package change, or a product modification, using a binary variable called a dummy variable. Dummy variables are coded 0 or 1, where 0 means that the policy is not in effect (not active) and 1 means that policy is in effect (active). Because simple linear regression is used, only one policy can be examined (the regression model contains only one dummy variable).

Consider that a package change is being planned for a product, and that in the product's sales history there have been two package changes. Graphical analysis reveals that the product sales tend to increase for a period of four weeks (spike in sales due to the attention that the new package attracts) and then settles back down to the average sales level prior to the package change. There is no evidence or rationale to suggest any different type of occurrence. The following formula is calculated with the dummy variable reflecting a t-statistic well above 2 (and therefore the relationship between the dummy variable and weekly product unit sales is statistically significant):

Weekly Product Units Sales = 25,000 + 5,000
(four-week period following new package introduction)

This equation suggests that during the fours weeks following the new package introduction, weekly unit sales increase by 5,000 units, corresponding to an incremental sales increase of 20,000 units due to the new package design. This increase is an estimate of sales impact based on the average effect shown by the previous two package changes. Because simple linear regression with dummy variables is being used, the forecast will be a constant sales figure in the first four weeks of the package change; that is, the forecast will be 30,000 unit sales per week. After these first four weeks, sales will settle back down to 25,000 unit sales per week. This type of analysis characterizes event modeling because the dummy variable is representing a particular event in the product's history.

Multiple Linear Regression

Multiple linear regression analysis develops an equation to express the linear effects of multiple variables simultaneously on the dependent variable. While the terminology of independent variable and dependent variable can be used, it also is managerially meaningful to employ the terminology of business drivers (e.g., advertising, coupon promotion, price) and a business outcome (e.g., sales). The general equation for multiple linear regression is $y = a + b1 \times 1 + b2 \times 2 + \ldots$, where y is the dependent variable, a is the y-intercept constant, $b1$ is the coefficient for variable $x1$, $b2$ is the coefficient for variable $x2$, and so on. Determining the significance of the independent variable's effect on the dependent variable is again based on statistical significance using the t-statistic, where t-statistic values above 2 or below -2 are judged as statistically significant, as previously discussed. Least squares estimation represents a popular approach for creating the multiple regression equation.

In addition to reviewing the t-statistics for each independent variable, it is useful to view the percent variation in the dependent variable that is being explained by the independent variables. This is done by evaluating the R-squared value for the regression equation, where the closer the R-squared value is to 1 (or 100 percent variation explained), the better the fit of the regression model. There are no set rules for an acceptable R-squared value; some low values, while not explaining a substantial portion of the variation of the dependent variable, may be managerially meaningful. The key is that at least one of the independent variables is found to reflect a statistically significant relationship with the dependent variable.

As an example, the simple linear regression equation could be made into a multiple linear regression model by adding a dummy variable representing a package change, as discussed in the previous example (both variables reflect statistically significant t-statistics where the t-statistic for price is below -2 and the t-statistic for the dummy variable is above 2):

New Product Sales in units = 105 – 6 (price in U.S. dollars)
+ 10 (four-week period following new package introduction)

Figure 6.1 **An Illustration of Multicollinearity**

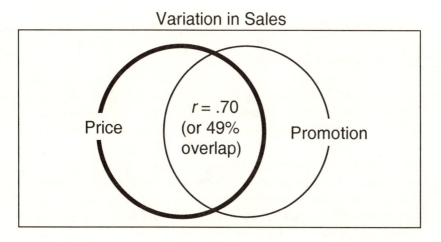

Note that the coefficients change when variables are added to the equation. This is because multiple regression coefficients are influenced by the relationships among the independent variables, as well as the relationship with the dependent variable. The relationships among independent variables in a multiple linear regression model are called multicollinearity. The goal of the forecast analyst is to maximize the strength of the relationship between a respective independent variable and the dependent variable, and minimize the strength of the relationships among the independent variables. Else erroneous coefficients, and correspondingly, flawed equations can result. In other words, the higher the multicollinearity between variables, the less unique contribution that an independent variable provides to the multiple regression equation. A rule of thumb is to keep the correlations between independent variables below .8 or 64 percent of the variation explained between any two independent variables.

For instance, if a regression equation included price and a promotion, and the correlation between these two variables was .7, it would suggest that the unique contribution by each variable is close to 50 percent. That is, price and the promotion overlap about half of each other in terms of the unique explanatory contribution that each variable provides to the dependent variable. While below the given rule of thumb, a correlation of .7 is still a borderline case for high multicollinearity. Refer to Figure 6.1 for a representative illustration of multicollinearity.

Guidelines for Linear Regression

When employing linear regression, regardless of whether simple or multiple in nature, the following guidelines must be adhered to:

- The independent variables and dependent variables have a linear relationship.
- The variation in the difference between actual and predicted values is the same for all fitted values of Y (which is called homoscedasticity).
- Residuals are normally distributed with a mean of 0.
- Successive observations of the dependent variable are uncorrelated (which is called autocorrelation).
- Independent variables are not highly correlated with each other (which is called multicollinearity).
- The dependent variable must be continuous and at least interval scale.

In addition to the above guidelines, the forecast analyst must be cognizant that regression is predicated on correlational relationships, and does not substantiate causation. As well, some relationships found to be statistically significant may lack sound reasoning behind why such a relationship should exist. Those relationships that cannot be explained soundly or are nonsensical in nature are referred to as spurious relationships and should be removed from the analysis.

Nonlinear Regression

The natural assumption of linear regression analyses is that relationships between the independent variables and dependent variable are linear. In some cases, the relationship cannot be assumed linear and so a nonlinear relationship may apply. Nonlinear regression is particularly applicable in modeling the life cycle of new products when using a variation of time series regression where time is the sole source for independent variables.

For example, a company was interested in establishing the shape of the life cycle for a technology product within its offerings portfolio and then using this equation to make a prediction about the shape of the life cycle for a forthcoming second-generation product. In applying this methodology, the assumptions were that the second-generation product will have the same market response as the first-generation product and that the product lives for both products will be equivalent. The life-cycle equation was derived using time specifically defined as the individual months 1 to 10 (designated by the numbers 1, 2, 3, . . . 10, respectively). As shown, a range of "higher-order" models was examined by modeling time to the nth power, where the linear model represented time to the power of 1, the quadratic model represented time to the power of 2 (squared), and the cubic model represented time to the power of three (cubed). Note that as higher-order models are examined, lower-order variables remain in the regression analyses, for example, the linear model has one independent variable; the quadratic model has two independent variables for linear and quadratic (squared) factors; and the cubic model has three independent variables for linear, quadratic, and cubic (cubed) factors. Higher-order models beyond the cubic model could have been examined by simply increasing the power applied to the time variable, however, experience suggests that linear, quadratic, and cubic models are usually sufficient. Table 6.1 illustrates each of these three models.

Reviewing regression analyses statistics like the t-statistic and R^2 determines which model is more appropriate in explaining the variation in life-cycle sales. As shown in Table 6.2, the linear model closely fits unit sales history, with the quadratic and cubic models showing incremental gains in R-squared (mostly because the addition of more independent variables naturally leads to better explanation). The issue to consider is whether an additional independent variable is statistically significant. In the case of the quadratic model, both independent variables are judged as statistically significant (t-stat$_{time^2}$ is close enough to 2 to be considered statistically significant). The cubic model contains one variable, t-stat$_{time}$, that is not close to a level of statistical significance. The results of these analyses suggest that the linear model or quadratic model will be sufficient; the quadratic model is favored due to its incrementally better R^2 statistic. Table 6.2 presents the projected sales figures for each of these two models.

Interestingly, the linear model is shown to have less forecast error (gives a more accurate prediction). This illustrates that explanation, accomplished by reviewing t-statistics and R^2, is not the same as predication, accomplished by calculating accuracy statistics like mean absolute percent error. The two are related, but there is not a one-to-one corre-

Table 6.1

An Example Comparing Linear, Quadratic, and Cubic Time Series Regression Models

Cumulative unit sales from first product	Linear model: time variable	Quadratic model: time variable	Cubic model: time variable
34	1	1	1
50	2	4	8
186	3	9	27
280	4	16	64
390	5	25	125
518	6	36	216
585	7	49	343
643	8	64	512
717	9	81	729
770	10	100	1,000
Model equation	Sales = −70 +89 (time)	Sales = −128 +118 (time) −2.6 (time^2)	Sales = −38 +38 (time) +15 (time^2) −1.05 (time^3)
t-statistics for the independent variables	$t\text{-stat}_{time} = 22.17$	$t\text{-stat}_{time} = 7.66$ $t\text{-stat}_{time2} = -1.94$	$t\text{-stat}_{time} = 1.08$ $t\text{-stat}_{time2} = 2.04$ $t\text{-stat}_{time3} = -2.44$
Model R-squared	98.4%	98.9%	99.4%

Table 6.2

Projected Sales Figures Using Linear and Quadratic Time Series Regression Models

Cumulative unit sales from first product	Projected sales using the linear model	Projected sales using the quadratic model
34	18	0
50	107	96
186	196	201
280	284	300
390	373	394
518	462	483
585	550	566
643	639	644
717	727	717
770	816	784
Mean absolute Percent error	20% error (80% accuracy)	26% error (74% accuracy)

Table 6.3

Evaluating Price Using a Nonlinear Regression Model

Proposed price ($)	Unit sales forecast
1.0	28,750
1.5	29,688
2.0	30,000
2.5	29,688
3.0	28,750
3.5	27,188
4.0	25,000

spondence because, as shown, the slightly lower R-squared model is more predictable. This is not always the case so both R-squared and forecast accuracy statistics should be calculated and examined.

A second application of nonlinear regression is in cases where independent variables reflect a nonlinear relationship with the dependent variable. For example, there are certain market cases where too low a price can reduce sales and too high a price also can reduce sales due to the customer seeing the low price as an indicator of low quality and the high price as too expensive. Consequently, there is a price threshold where sales will maintain or even grow. The following equation for a forthcoming new product illustrates this situation (assume all variables are statistically significant at 95 percent statistical confidence):

$$\text{Unit Sales} = 25{,}000 + 5000 \, (\text{price}) - 1250 \, (\text{price}^2)$$

Applying this equation to the price range of $1 to $4, $2 provides the maximum sales amount of 30,000 units and suggests that the $2 price should be adopted for the new product. Refer to Table 6.3.

Preference Regression

A variation of multiple linear regression is to examine customers' revealed preferences about a particular product category (e.g., grocery products, automobiles) and brands within that category. In doing so, the regression model will infer the importance weights to various given criteria and thereby suggest drivers for customers' preferences toward particular products.

Customer preference data can be collected several ways. Urban and Hauser (1993) suggest that customers can (1) allocate up to 100 points per product across a set of products to indicate their preference (similar to anchored importance measures), (2) allocate 100 points across a set of products with those most preferred given more points (similar to constant sum importance measures), (3) make paired comparisons across a set of given products, or (4) rank order a given set of products (and then rescale so that the highest ranked product is given the highest preference score). Attribute data on the product category would also be collected. To simplify the analyses, Urban and Hauser (1993) suggest taking the attribute data and using factor analysis to aggregate the data into factors. A factor score for each factor could then be inputted as an independent variable. The recommendation to use factor scores is predicated on the fact that factors scores will minimize multicollinearity while raw attribute data often is strongly correlated among itself.

An example of a preference regression model for cellular telephone preference is developed. A variety of attribute data is collected and through factor analysis is categorized into the two factors of size and functionality. The standardized coefficient for size is .45 and the standardized coefficient for functionality is .55, as reflected in the following preference regression model equation: Preference = *Constant* + .45 (size) + .55 (functionality). This regression model equation suggests that functionality has a stronger influence on cellular telephone preference. Though the analysis reveals that both size and functionality are important, if there must be a tradeoff, then that tradeoff should favor functionality. The developed model also can be employed for what-if analysis by inputting proposed product alterations to see the possible impact on product preference.

When conducting the regression analysis, the constant in the regression model can be ignored because it provides the scale for the model and is not used for relative comparisons. The coefficients for each factor are the important relative comparisons. Because the current example examines only two factors, the ratio of the two factors will give the slope of the ideal positioning vector and serves as a guide for future product design decisions. That is, one can plot the factor scores of the items evaluated and then overlay the slope suggested by this ratio to point to the preferred region to where future product designs should progress.

Logistic Regression

Logistic regression is applied to situations where the dependent variable is binary in nature, akin to a dummy variable coded 0 or 1. Such analysis is useful in understanding purchase versus nonpurchase behavior, and making predictions on the likelihood of whether a customer will purchase or not purchase a new product given specific input data. The statistical distinction of logistic regression is that the normal distribution cannot be used because of the dichotomous nature of the dependent variable and, thus, a binomial distribution is used instead. The dichotomous nature of the dependent variable also necessitates use of maximum likelihood versus least squares to estimate model coefficients. Individual coefficients for each independent variable cannot be assessed using t-statistics because the normal distribution does not apply. Instead, it is usual to substitute the Wald statistic, which is interpreted the same way as a t-statistic when logistic regression is used.

The outcome of a logistic regression is an estimate of the probability that a particular outcome will occur between 0 and 1. If the predicted probability of an outcome (likelihood of purchase) is greater than .5, then the prediction is yes, the outcome will occur. If the predicted probability of the outcome is less than .5, then the prediction is no, the outcome will not occur. Refer to the data in Table 6.4.

Evaluation of a logistic regression model is done by examining a likelihood value, in lieu of the R-squared statistic. The lower the likelihood value, the better the fit of the model to the given data. Predictability is assessed using classification tables to determine if the derived model correctly classified purchasers versus nonpurchasers, for example. The higher the percentage of data points correctly classified, the better the model in terms of its predictability. In Table 6.4, the projected purchase likelihoods for four out of five customers were correct, indicating a model accuracy of 80 percent. Guidelines for logistic regression suggest that models with a classification accuracy of above 50 percent are better than chance alone and therefore deemed acceptable. The level of 80 percent classification accuracy is considered well above chance, and so the model is considered acceptable, if not very acceptable.

Aside from customer analysis, logistic regression can be used to evaluate new product development projects. If a database on product development projects has been maintained, a regression model comparing successful projects (coded 1) versus unsuccessful projects (coded 0) can

Table 6.4

Logistic Regression Model Example

Customer	Purchase	Annual income	Price	Predicted probability of purchase (%)	Projected purchase
1	0 (No)	62	30	68	Yes
2	1 (Yes)	95	20	99	Yes
3	1 (Yes)	56	20	74	Yes
4	0 (No)	50	30	32	No
5	0 (No)	45	30	20	No

$$p(\text{purchase}) = \frac{e^{-3.8024 + (-.105 \times \text{Price}) + (.124 \times \text{Income})}}{1 + e^{-3.8024 + (-105 \times \text{Price}) + (.124 \times \text{Income})}}$$

be created. This model will assist in verifying which project-related data correlates to project success (typically a project that achieves a successful product launch). If such a database does not exist, it may be prudent to begin collecting product development project data. Such data could include gate deliverables from the project team and gate review paperwork from the review team. Analysis of these data would be possible after enough data is collected. The guideline is five cases per independent variable: if five project criteria are tracked through gates, then a history on twenty-five project cases would be recommended. Creation of such a logistic regression model within a company parallels the scoring model called New Prod™, which is an empirically derived, cross-industry model that evaluates the profile of a new product project against its success criteria. These criteria are based on experiences and outcomes of hundreds of previous new product launches, and include measures of synergy, differential advantage, market attractiveness, and project familiarity. See Cooper (1993) for further information on the New Prod™ model.

Final Comments on Regression Analyses

As one should surmise from the discussion in this chapter, simple linear regression is less sophisticated than the subsequently discussed regression analyses of multiple linear regression, nonlinear regression, preference regression, and logistic regression. Still, all regression analyses are sophisticated in nature, and this chapter's discussion of the topic has only touched on a limited number of issues involved with developing and validating any regression model. Those wishing to use regression analysis are strongly urged to reference sources for refreshing one's statistical skills, if not to gain a fuller understanding of regression analysis and its proper application (examples of references include Hair et al. 1998, Mason and Lind 1996, and Neter et al. 1996).

Key Concepts

Correlation
Simple Linear Regression
Multiple Linear Regression
Nonlinear Regression
Preference Regression
Logistic Regression

Discussion Questions

1. What information does a correlation provide?
2. What is the difference between simple linear regression and multiple linear regression?
3. What are some critical assumptions when employing linear regression?
4. What is a dummy variable when used with regression analysis?
5. What is the difference between preference regression and logistic regression?

Part III

Managerial Considerations for Applied New Product Forecasting

Excellence is an art won by training and habituation.
Aristotle, Greek Philosopher (384–322 BCE)

Forecasting new products is both art and science. The science of new product forecasting stems from the application of the previously discussed forecasting techniques. The art stems from understanding and properly managing the issues inherent to new product forecasting. Chapter 7 introduces special topics that deserve special attention during the new product forecasting endeavor. These include the launch phenomenon, cannibalization, supercession, and end-of-life planning. Chapter 8 then follows with industry benchmarks for better and best practices for new product forecasting. Such benchmarks serve as guidelines and guideposts to underlie one's continuous improvement efforts toward proficient and meaningful new product forecasting.

7

Special Topics in New Product Forecasting

The commitment to launch is normally assured once a product enters the commercialization and launch phase. New product forecasting is an important part of and subsumed within launch, which is also referred to as new product introduction. The present chapter discusses the issues of launch, launch planning, and details for a proper launch control protocol. Also discussed are the issues of cannibalization and supercession, which are key elements of not only new product planning, but life-cycle planning.

Understanding the Launch Phenomenon

Everett Rogers's diffusion of innovations theory is useful for understanding the launch phenomenon (see Rogers 1995). Originally developed in the 1950s within the context of agricultural products, his theory has been used to explain launch and product acceptance across multiple product contexts. Diffusion of innovations theory attempts to explain the drivers behind individuals' decisions to adopt (purchase) or reject (not purchase) a new product. The accumulation of all individual adoption processes is referred to as diffusion. Adoption and diffusion also can be distinguished by realizing that customers adopt products and products diffuse into the marketplace.

Rogers's work indicates that in general, consumers—whether individual or business-to-business in nature, transition through a five-stage adoption process:

Stage 1: Knowledge—the customer receives physical or social stimuli and recognizes that a problem or shortcoming exists.

Stage 2: Persuasion—the customer weighs the risks versus the benefits of the new product to gauge whether the new product is worth it.

Stage 3: Decision—the consumer decides to either adopt or reject the new product. If adoption is the outcome, the consumer has made the decision to actively pursue acquiring the new product. If rejection is the outcome, two types of rejection are possible: active rejection, which is when the consumer considers adoption, and may even try the product, but decide not to adopt; passive rejection, which is when the customer never considers use of the product (also referred to as nonadoption).

Stage 4: Implementation—driven by the decision to adopt, the consumer will make the effort to purchase and put the product to use.

Stage 5: Confirmation—customers will seek reinforcement of the innovation decision to reduce possible cognitive dissonance, i.e., second thoughts about the purchase.

Based on these five stages, companies can target a particular marketing/promotion campaign and facilitate the consumer's progression through the respective stage favoring the new product. The specific marketing/promotion materials under control of the company are awareness, trial, availability, and repeat, which combined represent the ATAR model discussed in chapter 3. In fact, the ATAR model has strong ties to Rogers's adoption model, if not parallel ties. The relationship between Rogers's adoption model and the ATAR model is shown in Figure 7.1.

As presented, awareness can be employed to pose a problem to the consumer and stimulate thinking in favor of the new product. Awareness also can provide information to assist in weighing risks and benefits. Particular attention should focus on awareness to let customers know about the company and the new product offering. Along with advertising and publicity postlaunch, companies can employ preannouncements prior to launch to stimulate knowledge and persuasion via awareness.

Various initiatives regarding trial such as demonstrations and samples encourage consumers to make a favorable decision, so particular interest should focus on having customers try the new product. Promotions

Figure 7.1 **The Adoption Process and the ATAR Model**

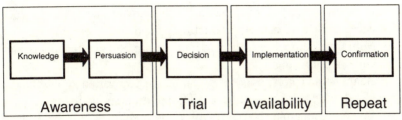

that generate self-interest or interest that is vicarious in nature (try the product because others have tried the product) are two options. In the course of attempting to drive trial, the company must overcome the following barriers to trial: lack of interest in the product, lack of belief in the product, rejection due to something negative about the product, complacency about the new product, competition, doubts about whether trying the product is worthwhile, lack of usage opportunities, product cost, customer loyalty to other products, and customers' perceived risk of rejection or pending product failure.

Availability is controlled by the company through market channel presence and the number of selling outlets where the new product will be sold. If a consumer chooses to purchase the new product but cannot locate it, a lost sale is likely. To ensure availability, the company should make sure that distributors, dealers, and resellers can offer your product to the market. Use of trade discounts and trade incentives can be employed as vehicles to ensure that channel partners will carry the new product and sustain the level of availability necessary to meet financial targets and forecasts.

Repeat initiatives like coupons toward a second purchase can be useful in reducing perceived risks in buying the new product and reduce barriers to subsequent purchases by the consumer. Contracts may be useful for getting repurchase in business-to-business channels.

In addition to the five stages of adoption, Rogers (1995) indicates that five key product characteristics can facilitate the adoption process, especially in the persuasion stage, leading to adoption by consumers and overall market diffusion. The prescription is to consider how the new product offering can reflect these characteristics, if not integrate them into the product design and/or marketing plan. These product/ service characteristics include:

- Reflect a relative advantage: the new product must be superior to current product offerings.
- Have compatibility with the customer's environment: the product needs to fit with current product usage and customer activity.
- Minimize complexity: the product should be easy to understand and not confusing.
- Be divisible (offer trials): if possible, the innovation should be divided into trial samples; have trial opportunities available.
- Be communicable (be observable): the product should be easy to communicate, not only in terms of promoting the product, but also in terms of customer word-of-mouth; the product also should be able to be observed publicly.

The new product forecasting team should examine the new product along these characteristics when conducting various types of consumer testing and evaluating the proposed marketing plan. New products that reflect a high relative advantage, have strong compatibility, minimize perceived complexity, can be divided into trial offerings, and can more readily communicate features and benefits are more likely to have higher sales levels. These characteristics also can be introduced as part of the assumption accumulation process to frame discussions of the new product's forecast.

An additional contribution of diffusion theory is the recognition that the marketplace does not normally reflect 100 percent market saturation immediately. Rather, the cumulative trajectory to market saturation is in the form of an S-shaped curved, as shown by the Bass model (discussed in chapter 5). Rogers's (1995) work further points out that adoption is a staggered phenomenon across customers with different types of consumers adopting the new product at different points in time. As previously mentioned in chapter 3, these consumers can be categorized into five general types of adopters. The first group to purchase a new product is called the innovators or lead users. Innovators generally make up 2.5 percent of the market. Early adopters are the second category of purchasers and comprise 13.5 percent of the market. Together innovators and early adopters serve as opinion leaders for the rest of consumers, who represent the "main market." The early majority is the third group of consumers and makes up 34 percent of the market. The late majority is the fourth group of consumers and represents another 34 percent of the market. The remaining 16 percent of the market are referred to as the laggards category and include consumers who are characteristically re-

Figure 7.2 **Adopter Categories**

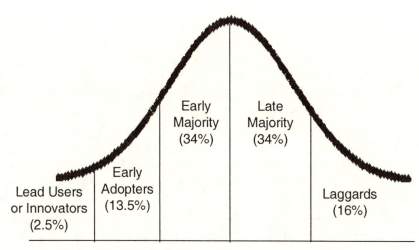

sistant to change and to new technology. (Refer to Figure 7.2.)

These percentages can be useful for not only conceptualizing market segments, but also for estimating market penetration rates of new products. For example, forecasts for a new emerging technology suggest a market potential of 100,000 units, but because this technology is revolutionary in nature, conceivably only the "innovators" and "early adopters" will purchase the product in the first year. The total market potential forecast therefore should be discounted 16 percent to suggest a market potential of 16,000 units in the first year. If the projected market share for the company is 20 percent of this market potential, then the sales potential estimate is 3,200 unit sales.

The Launch Cycle

Launch actually can be conceived as a cycle that proceeds in four phases: (1) prelaunch preparation, (2) announcement, (3) beachhead, and (4) early growth (see Figure 7.3). Prelaunch preparation comprises the activities that precede the actual point at which the product is officially offered for sale in the market. These activities typically will include making preannouncements (public company statements about the pending launch of the product), building marketing capability, establishing service capability, promoting the new product via public relations, and filling the distribution pipeline. The construction of a launch control protocol and tying it

Figure 7.3 **The Launch Cycle**

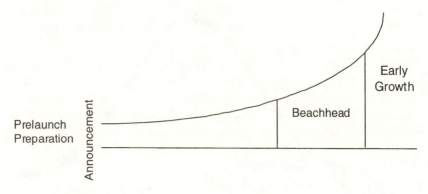

to the launch scorecard also occur during prelaunch preparation. All of these activities in total have the purpose of building excitement and ensuring that the company is ready to meet expected market demand.

Announcement is the next point in the launch cycle and is of a short duration. By definition, announcement is the point at which the product is officially offered to the complete market. It is at the point of announcement that all decisions are finalized.

The third phase is beachhead. Here efforts focus on achieving market awareness and generating an initial stream of sales.

The fourth phase of launch is early growth. Hopefully, sales will grow as interest in the new product grows. If sales are not growing, a decision needs to be made quickly. There are five decision options: (1) increase spending; (2) revise the launch/marketing strategy; (3) revise the product (a costly, timely, and potentially risky endeavor); (4) pull the product temporarily from the marketplace (a risky option, which often does not to lead to success the second time around); or (5) abandon the product (given the amount of resources expensed during the product development process, this option should be considered the last option). Note that options 1 and 2 should be considered initially. If these two options do not work, then options 3, 4, and 5 should be taken, with option 5 representing the last resort/final option.

Prelaunch Preparation: Launch Control Protocol

The launch control protocol is an important, useful tool. In the same vein as the product protocol during the technical development phase, the launch protocol is used to support monitor and control activities during the launch cycle. The launch control protocol identifies key "deliverables" or success measures during product launch. Such measures can correspond to a variety of issues, including sales volume, profitability, market awareness, or other designated issue. Along with these measures, the launch control protocol establishes trigger points to indicate at what point action needs to be taken; such trigger points represent precursors of pending problems during launch. The launch control protocol further specifies what type of action should be taken beforehand to avoid unnecessary confusion and brash "fire-fighting."

Constructing a launch control protocol follows four steps. The first step is to identify potential problems that might occur during a particular product's launch. Three ways to identify such problems include reviewing the situation analysis from the marketing plan to outline potential threats, looking at the company's product launch history to indicate problems from previous product launches, and role-playing. Role-playing is especially powerful for revealing problems, where employees portray various channel members and competitors. In fact, one company found that after several iterations of a role-playing exercise, they had successfully iterated a list of foreseeable problems and established remedies for these problems. As it turned out, the company was able to stay one step ahead of competitors because they had foreseen competitor responses and potential market problems.

The second step in a launch control protocol is to select the problems that should be monitored and controlled. Selection should be based on the impact of the potential problem to the commercial success of the respective products. Those problems that can severely hamper success should be selected.

The third step in a launch control protocol is to design a system for monitoring and controlling each of the selected problems. To do this, it is necessary to first identify a measurable variable that corresponds to each problem. For example, if one of the selected problems was "sales lower than expected," two possible variables to measure would be unit sales volume or revenue sales volume. It is necessary to specify which variable is most appropriate to get at the selected problem: unit sales, revenue sales, or both. In addition to identifying the measurable variable, it is necessary to identify the trigger point for that variable. If "sales lower than expected" is the problem, what would represent this situation —unit sales less than 100,000 units? revenue sales less than $1,000,000? It is neces-

Figure 7.4 **Launch Control Protocol Example**

Potential Problem	Tracking	Contingency Plan
Customers are not making trial purchases of the new product as expected.	Look at POS reports. Minimum, 100 purchases monthly per retail outlet are expected.	Install point-of-purchase (POP) displays.
Competitor may have similar new product.	Difficult to track, but conduct surveys with retailers and final consumers.	Offer 2 for 1 program. Consider bundling new product with other products.

sary to specify the boundary at which a problem should be recognized.

The fourth step in a launch control protocol is to develop remedies or contingency plans for each of the selected problems. Essentially, these remedies or contingency plans would set out a course of action that the company would undertake in the event that the problem arose. Figure 7.4 presents a sample of a launch control protocol. As shown, the problem of "customers are not making trial purchases of the new product as expected" is tracked by point-of-sale (POS) data with the trigger point of less than 100 unit purchases per retail outlet per month signifying a problem. The remedy for the problem is implementation of point-of-purchase (POP) displays.

During the launch control protocol, some consideration should be given to unforeseen and nontrackable problems. Obviously, these will be difficult to conceive, but consideration beforehand may help identify a potential problem area. In a good launch control protocol, general contingencies (courses of action) regarding what to do in the case that something not specified in the launch control protocol occurs will alleviate confusion. In this way, the launch team knows ahead of time what they may need to do just in case something unexpected does happen.

Launch Tracking and the Launch Scorecard

The metrics and tracking signals identified in the launch control protocol are natural components for the launch scorecard. If a common new product forecasting template can be established for use with all types of new products, a common set of critical assumptions will be predetermined. Subsequently, these critical assumptions would be tracked through

Figure 7.5   **Launch Scorecard as Part of the Regular
S&OP Meeting Report**

Score
55.3%

Retail Market New Products
Fiscal Period 8

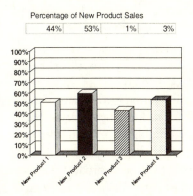

Percentage of New Product Sales

| 44% | 53% | 1% | 3% |

- Key Account did not switch from Original Product to New Product 1 as assumed and assured

- Forecast override for New Product 2 added unnecessary optimism

- Supply problem with special packaging of New Product 3

- Slower than expected market uptake for New Product 4

the new product development process and become the foundation of the launch scorecard.

Variations of the launch scorecard will exist, depending on each company situation. Rather than have additional paperwork, the launch scorecard can be integrated into the monthly Sales and Operations Planning (S&OP) report (also called the monthly S&OP deck in some companies). Metrics, emerging issues, and the reasons for these emerging issues will be listed. Attuning the executive S&OP team to these data ensures that detrimental issues are remedied, the new product receives the proper attention and resources, and the new product does not interfere with the success of other products and overall company operations. As suggested in Figure 7.5, the launch scorecard can be a normal part of the regular S&OP documentation. This will provide visibility to all new products during their launch period.

Special New Product Forecasting Issues

Issues of cannibalization, supercession, and end-of-life planning are integral to the new product introduction discussions. Unfortunately, there is no one set course or methodology for addressing these. Rather, the forecaster should be aware of the issues involved and possible strategies that may be employed to address the respective issues during new product forecasting and new product introduction.

Cannibalization

Cannibalization is "the process by which a new product gains sales by diverting them from an existing product" (Heskett 1976, p. 581). Unfortunately, there is no clear-cut means to identify cannibalization. One approach is to use the brand-switching matrix (as discussed in chapter 3), where the new product is one of the likely competitors.

Another approach for estimating cannibalization is the share order effects (SOE) model (see Lomax et al. 1997). The SOE model states that all brands lose share to the new product entrant in direct proportion to their size before the launch. This means that an assumption must be made a priori regarding the market share to be taken by the new product. The new product's market share is then used to adjust current shares held by products already in the market, including the company's current products.

For example, a new product is envisioned to take a 5 percent share within the first year against Products A, B, and C, which have 20 percent, 30 percent, and 50 percent current market share, respectively. Applying the share order effects model, the new product will gain a 5 percent market share, resulting in Product A dropping to a 19 percent market share [20% x ((100%–5%)/100%)], Product B dropping to a 28.5 percent share [30% x ((100%–5%)/100%)], and Product C dropping to a 47.5 percent share [50% x ((100%–5%)/100%)].

A third approach is to apply order of entry (OE) matrices, commonly employed in the pharmaceutical industry. These data matrices suggest what market share is likely to be based on a product's order of entry. For example, Figure 7.6 indicates that in the case of two competitors, the first-to-market entry will sustain a 58.48 percent market share and the second-to-market entry will gain a 41.52 percent market share. While useful for conceptualizing possible cannibalization effects, actual results have found variability in the accuracy of predicted market share, particularly if later entries are implementing more expansive and well-funded marketing campaigns versus that which was used to support the first-to-market entry or other early market entries. There are also a number of cases where the second and later market entries are "second but

Figure 7.6   Order of Entry Matrix (%)

	1	2	3	4	5	6	7	8	9	10	11
1	100.00										
2	58.48	41.52									
3	43.64	30.99	25.37								
4	35.77	25.40	20.79	18.04							
5	30.80	21.87	17.90	15.53	13.91						
6	27.32	19.40	15.88	13.78	12.34	11.28					
7	24.74	17.57	14.38	12.47	11.17	10.21	9.46				
8	22.72	16.14	13.21	11.46	10.26	9.38	8.69	8.14			
9	21.10	14.99	12.27	10.64	9.53	8.71	8.07	7.56	7.13		
10	19.77	14.04	11.49	9.97	8.93	8.16	7.56	7.08	6.68	6.34	
11	18.64	13.24	10.83	9.40	8.42	7.69	7.13	6.67	6.30	5.98	5.70
12	17.67	12.55	10.27	8.91	7.98	7.29	6.76	6.33	5.97	5.67	5.41
13	16.84	11.96	9.79	8.49	7.60	6.95	6.44	6.03	5.69	5.40	5.15
14	16.10	11.43	9.36	8.12	7.27	6.64	6.16	5.76	5.44	5.16	4.93
15	15.45	10.97	8.98	7.79	6.98	6.38	5.91	5.53	5.22	4.95	4.73
16	14.86	10.55	8.64	7.49	6.71	6.13	5.68	5.32	5.02	4.77	4.55
17	14.34	10.18	8.33	7.23	6.48	5.92	5.48	5.13	4.84	4.60	4.39
18	13.86	9.84	8.06	6.99	6.26	5.72	5.30	4.96	4.68	4.45	4.24
19	13.43	9.53	7.80	6.77	6.06	5.54	5.14	4.81	4.54	4.31	4.11
20	13.03	9.25	7.57	6.57	5.88	5.38	4.98	4.66	4.40	4.18	3.99
21	12.66	8.99	7.36	6.38	5.72	5.23	4.84	4.53	4.28	4.06	3.87
22	12.32	8.75	7.16	6.21	5.56	5.09	4.71	4.41	4.16	3.95	3.77
23	12.01	8.53	6.98	6.05	5.42	4.96	4.59	4.30	4.06	3.85	3.67
24	11.71	8.32	6.81	5.91	5.29	4.84	4.48	4.19	3.96	3.76	3.58
25	11.44	8.12	6.65	5.77	5.17	4.72	4.38	4.10	3.87	3.67	3.50

Figure 7.7 **Technology S-Curve Roadmaps: An Example of Supercession**

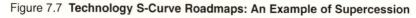
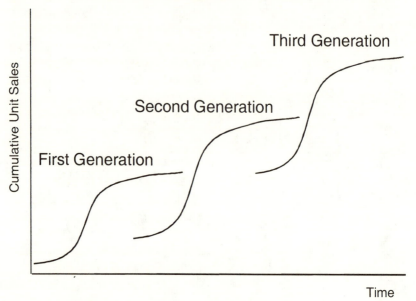

better" product offerings, thereby cannibalizing market entries and se-
curing a dominant share.

Supercession

Supercession is the process by which one product replaces another product. Supercession is the process by which a next-generation product replaces the current-generation product, such as in the technology sector.
Typical techniques used to estimate the supercession phenomenon are
looks-like analyses, where sales from the current generation are used as
a surrogate baseline forecast for the new generation, augmented by possible promotional events. Technology S-curves, akin to diffusion models, also are used to plan when next-generation technologies should be
launched, leading to a technology roadmap of multiple S-curves over-
laid on each other. Refer to Figure 7.7.

End-of-Life Planning

While not new product forecasting inherently, end-of-life planning is
necessary, especially if supercession will take place. Even if supercession

is not an issue, a product life expectancy should be considered for the given product offering. Specific activities can then be put in place to ensure that all inventory of the product is sold upon the product's official termination. End-of-life planning includes pricing strategy and scheduling when to turn off part procurement. Spare-parts forecasting is particularly an issue in end-of-life planning in the case of mechanized equipment because often such products continue to be used far beyond the given product life.

New Product Inventory Planning Versus New Product Forecasting

In some cases, new products just cannot be forecast due to inherent variability or uncertainty in the marketplace. While a baseline forecast is still necessary for these problematic new products, the forecast is greatly supplemented by safety stock derived through a set of inventory management policies to ensure product availability. This may seem advantageous, but it is usually better to have a more meaningful (and hopefully accurate) forecast, versus loading and sitting on inventory from the cost perspective—especially when volumes of the new product will lock up major resources and production capacity. All said, reliance on inventory planning versus forecasting is often more appropriate when new products will reflect lower volume or intermittent demand.

Two general inventory control models exist, with one type of model based on ordering at set time intervals and the other type of model based on ordering set amounts of inventory as the need arises. The former type is "event-triggered," which means that when a product's inventory reaches a specified reorder level, an "ordering event" is "triggered." This event may take place any time, depending on demand and level of inventory on-hand, and the amount of inventory ordered is a prespecified amount. The latter type of model is "time-triggered," meaning that the placing of orders is limited to a predetermined time period so that the passage of time "triggers" the model. The amount of inventory ordered is the difference between current inventory levels and the required inventory level. Choice to pursue either model is based on holding costs, setup costs, ordering costs, stockout costs, and necessary customer service levels. In comparing the two systems, research has found that the fixed time period review approach will generally require a larger amount of inventory than the fixed order quantity approach (Chase and Aquilano 1985).

Among the simpler fixed order quantity approaches is the Kanban approach, which is a popular reorder policy and one commonly associated with just-in-time production and lean production. This very specialized reorder policy is predicated on the use of two standardized lot size case/containers. When there is only one case/container in stock, a flag or signal (called a Kanban) is indicated to alert the need to order one more case. That is, when one case is withdrawn, a reorder point is reached and an ordering event is triggered. There is at least one case in stock at all times.

The decision to rely on an inventory management approach is predicated mostly on cost factors, but one must be mindful of whether there is ample space for the inventory. In addition, lead time for the ordered product to arrive must be within an acceptable time frame so as to not interrupt the ability to sustain product availability and satisfy customer demand. Some lead time for products, especially U.S.-based products with components from countries like China, have lead times as long as six months, which makes use of an inventory planning policy less attractive and the company strongly reliant on the new product forecasting process.

Key Concepts

Launch
Cannibalization
Supercession
End-of-Life Planning
Inventory Planning versus New Product Forecasting

Discussion Questions

1. What are the four phases of the launch cycle?
2. What are some appropriate metrics for a launch scorecard?
3. How might one assess cannibalization?
4. How is supercession and end-of-life planning related?
5. When would inventory planning be appropriate in lieu of holding firm to new product forecasting?

8

New Product Forecasting Benchmarks

Many articles on the subject of new product forecasting have been illustrations of specific forecasting techniques, often representing sophisticated statistical methodologies (e.g., Hardie, Fader, and Wisniewski 1998; Jain, Mahajan, and Muller 1995; Ozer 1999; Ram and Ram 1996; Rao 1985). A significant number of the remaining articles have been normative in nature, prescribing the need for continued study on the topic of new product forecasting for the sake of improving prediction capabilities (e.g., Armstrong 1996; Mahajan and Wind 1992). While this literature is valuable and offers insights into the new product forecasting effort, only a handful of articles have empirically examined managerial practices related to new product forecasting management to provide industry benchmark data. In an effort to provide such data, the Product Development and Management Association (PDMA) sponsored a benchmarking study on new product forecasting in 1999, with results reported in 2002 (see Kahn 2002). The study presents literature insights on new product forecasting, results of the PDMA benchmarking study, and observations from company experiences to help organize and outline thinking around applied new product forecasting. The end goal of the current chapter is to distinguish what "meaningful," successful *applied new product forecasting* should really mean.

Review of Literature on New Product Forecasting Practices

Aside from discussing particular forecasting techniques, literature has intensely discussed the topic of new product forecasting accuracy. For example, studying fifty-three products across sixteen firms, Tull (1967) reported that the mean forecast error was 53 percent. Studying the accuracy of forecasting profit, Beardsley and Mansfield (1978) found that it took four to five years after new product launch for a company to estimate discounted profits reasonably well. And Shelley and Wheeler (1991), who investigated market forecasts for the high-technology products of personal computer, artificial intelligence, and fiber-optics, found that the average ratio between actual sales and forecasted sales was .79 in the first year, .60 in the second year, .51 in the third year, .46 in the fourth year, and .41 in the fifth year.

Because of such relatively low accuracy associated with new product forecasting, Gartner and Thomas (1993) conducted a study to examine and identify underlying factors contributing to such forecast error within the context of new computer software firms. Their results suggest that industry marketing experience, more attention and resources directed toward new product forecasting, the use of personal data sources, and the use of more techniques all correspond to improved forecast accuracy. While not controllable per se, less market turbulence also was found to correspond to improved forecast accuracy. Based on these results, the following guidelines for generating more accurate new product forecasts were given:

> (1) recognize the importance of the new product forecasting task and develop a commitment (which includes financial resources) commensurate with the importance of the task to improve forecasts; (2) select new product forecasting data sources that bring the forecaster closer to the consumer (e.g., personal interviews, product demonstrations, focus groups); (3) use more than one method in combination throughout the product development process to develop forecasts; and (4) anticipate the volatility of the market to be entered and the behaviors of buyers within it as input to the new product forecasts. (Gartner and Thomas 1993, p. 48)

Lynn, Schnaars, and Skov (1999) conducted a study comparing the use of new product forecasting techniques by industrial high-technology businesses versus industrial low-technology businesses. Their analysis of seventy-six industrial new product projects found that successful high-tech industrial projects tended to rely more on the internal qualitative forecasting techniques of internal expert judgment and internal brainstorming versus unsuccessful high-tech industrial projects. Successful low-tech industrial projects tended to rely more on the traditional market research methods of one-on-one interviews with salespeople, surveys of buyers intentions, and formal surveys of customers. Results further suggested that successful firms, whether high-tech or low-tech, employed more new product forecasting techniques than unsuccessful firms. This latter finding corresponds to Gartner and Thomas's (1993) finding that use of more techniques corresponds to greater forecast accuracy.

Another set of new product forecasting literature has promoted diffusion models and their applicability to new product forecasting (e.g., Wind, Mahajan, and Cardozo 1981; Mahajan and Wind 1986; Mahajan, Muller, and Bass 1990; Morrison 1996, 1999). Unfortunately, empirical research has suggested that there is very limited use of diffusion models in industrial/business settings (Mahajan and Wind 1986; Goldner and Tellis 1998). One reason for this may be that diffusion models are sophisticated statistical models, which require expertise that most new product practitioners do not have. Another reason is the poor track record of diffusion models in actually predicting sales more accurately than other methods (Goldner and Tellis 1998).

New Product Forecasting Benchmarks

Through its 1999 sponsored research program, the PDMA commissioned a new product forecasting benchmarking study to identify current industry practices and attempt to identify preferable, if not better, practices related to new product forecasting. Such practices included department involvement in the new product forecasting effort, technique usage, and new product forecast accuracy. The study also investigated if accuracy, forecast time horizon, and forecasting technique usage might differ across different types of new products, that is, cost reductions, product improvements, line extensions, market extensions, new category entries, and new-to-the-world products? Additional analyses were undertaken to investigate possible differences between consumer and industrial firms to reveal any striking differences.

Methodology

Managers associated with the PDMA, the Institute of Business Forecasting (IBF), and a university-based marketing analysis consortium served as the respondents for the PDMA benchmarking study. The combined dataset, which was collected in 2000, comprised a total of 168

Table 8.1

Where the New Product Forecasting Function Resides

Department	Primarily responsible for new product forecasting (% of respondents) (n = 144)	Average level of involvement* (n = 144)
Marketing	62	4.29
		(s = 1.10)
Sales	13	3.61
		(s = 1.31)
Sales Forecasting	10	3.50
		(s = 1.50)
Finance	6	2.22
		(s = 1.26)
Market Research	3	3.34
		(s = 1.46)
R&D	3	2.92
		(s = 1.46)
Manufacturing	2	2.34
		(s = 1.36)
Logistics/Distribution	1	2.04
		(s = 1.28)

Notes: Involvement was assessed using a 1 to 5 scale, where 1 = "Does Not Partici-pate" to 5 = "Highly Involved."
n = sample size
s = standard deviation

respondents from a cross-section of industries that included automotive products, medical products, health and beauty products, construction equipment, and electronics—to name a few. A little more than half of the companies were strictly consumer market-focused (54 percent), while roughly a third (34 percent) of responding companies were strictly focused on the business-to-business market. The remaining companies characterized themselves as an equal mix of consumer and business-to-business products/services. The effective survey response rate across the three sets of data was 21 percent.

New Product Forecasting Practices Across All Firms

Almost two-thirds (62 percent) of respondents indicated that the marketing department is primarily responsible for the new product forecasting function (see Table 8.1). This shows the marketing department to be the predominant department responsible for the new product forecasting function. Only two other departments reflected greater than 10 percent of respondents: the sales department was responsible for new product forecasting in 13 percent of the cases, and the sales forecasting department was responsible for new product forecasting in 10 percent of the cases.

The level of participation by these three departments is high. Marketing is very much involved in the new product forecasting process, and is the most involved department. Sales and sales forecasting departments also are more involved in the new product forecasting process than other departments besides marketing. Market research is more involved in the new product forecasting process as well. This indicates that market research plays an important role in new product forecasting, but is not typically responsible for the new product forecasting function.

Survey recipients were asked to indicate technique usage across six types of new products, corresponding to Crawford's list of new product types (Crawford and Di Benedetto 2000). These included cost reductions (reduced cost or reduced price versions of the product for the existing market); product improvements (new, improved versions of existing products/services, targeted to the current market); line extensions (incremental innovations added to existing product lines and targeted to the current market); market extensions (taking existing products/services to new markets); new category entries (new-to-the-company product and new-to-the-company market, but not new to the general market); and new-to-the-world (radically different products/ services versus current offerings and markets served). To guide survey recipients, a list of twenty common sales forecasting techniques compiled from a variety of sales forecasting and technological forecasting sources (e.g., Makridakis et al. 1983; Mentzer and Kahn 1995) was provided. Those completing the survey also were give the option of an "other" category, which allowed the writing in of forecasting techniques not listed.

As shown in Table 8.2, the more popular new product forecasting techniques (those techniques receiving greater than 10 percent average usage across the six types of new products) were customer/market research, jury of executive opinion, sales force composite method, looks-like analysis, trend line analysis, moving average, and scenario analysis. These results correspond to Lynn, Schnaars, and Skov (1999), who had

Table 8.2

Use of New Product Forecasting Techniques by All Responding Firms (%)

Forecasting technique	Average use across all types of new products	CR (n = 45)	PI (n = 117)	LE (n = 112)	ME (n = 108)	NCE (n = 58)	NTW (n = 103)
Customer/market research	57	42	54	54	57	71	62
Jury of executive opinion	44	49	38	40	45	53	48
Sales force composite	39	38	38	46	41	40	29
Looks-like analysis	30	22	26	32	32	36	29
Trend line analysis	19	29	25	18	18	14	14
Moving average	15	24	17	17	14	10	11
Scenario analysis	14	7	14	11	15	19	18
Exponential smoothing techniques	10	7	13	15	11	3	7
Experience curves	10	18	11	10	8	7	8
Market analysis model (including the ATAR model)	10	4	9	8	9	17	12
Delphi method	8	9	8	8	6	10	9
Linear regression	7	9	9	9	6	0	5
Decision trees	7	13	4	3	6	9	10
Simulation	5	0	6	4	6	5	8
Expert systems	4	4	6	4	4	0	3

	CR	PI	LE	ME	NCE	NTW
Other	3	2	4	2	5	3
Nonlinear regression	2	1	2	3	2	1
Diffusion models	2	0	1	2	3	3
Precursor curves (correlation method)	1	1	2	0	0	0
Box-Jenkins techniques (ARMA/ARIMA)	1	2	0	2	0	0
Neural networks	0	0	0	0	0	0
Average number of techniques employed	2.80 ($s = 1.56$)	2.83 ($s = 1.84$)	2.83 ($s = 1.93$)	2.84 ($s = 1.95$)	3.00 ($s = 1.71$)	2.75 ($s = 1.96$)

Notes:

CR = cost reductions: reduced cost or price versions of the product for the existing market;

PI = product improvements: new, improved versions of existing products/services, targeted to the current market;

LE = line extensions: incremental innovations added to existing product lines and targeted to the current market;

ME = market extensions: taking existing products/services to new markets;

NCE = new category entries: new-to-the-company product and new-to-the-company market, but not new to the general market;

NTW = new-to-the-world products: radically different products/services versus current offerings and markets served.

Average use = a weighted average across the six types of new products.

n = sample size

s = standard deviation

Note that multiple responses were allowed.

Table 8.3

**Percent of Forecast Accuracy and Forecast Horizon for
New Product Forecasts**

Type of new product	Average percent accuracy achieved (standard deviation, sample size)	Forecast horizon in months (standard deviation, sample size)
Cost reductions	71.62	21.15
	($s = 22.46$, $n = 29$)	($s = 21.15$, $n = 40$)
Product improvements	64.88	19.96
	($s = 23.63$, $n = 45$)	($s = 18.20$, $n = 102$)
Line extensions	62.76	20.84
	($s = 22.25$, $n = 45$)	($s = 18.58$, $n = 97$)
Market extensions	54.33	23.58
	($s = 24.02$, $n = 42$)	($s = 21.26$, $n = 93$)
New category entries (new-to-the-company)	46.83	34.56
	($s = 24.31$, $n = 30$)	($s = 35.21$, $n = 45$)
New-to-the-world	40.36	36.08
	($s = 24.72$, $n = 39$)	($s = 35.96$, $n = 93$)

Notes:
n = sample size
s = standard deviation

suggested that managers prefer to rely on judgment and market research techniques versus traditional sales forecasting techniques like time series analysis and regression. Such correspondence is interesting in light of the fact that there are a number of quantitative techniques that literature espouses. Forecasting executives nonetheless show a strong preference toward less sophisticated, qualitative forecasting techniques like jury of executive opinion, sales force composite method, and looks-like analysis, along with a preference toward customer/market research, which may be quantitative or qualitative in nature. It is also interesting to observe that these techniques appear to be somewhat equally applied across the different types of new products, which suggests that new product forecasters commonly employ qualitative forecasting techniques along with market research, regardless of the type of new product. Results further show that on average, companies use about three techniques when forecasting each of the six types of new products. This latter finding supports research that indicates new product forecasting to be a process that comprises more than one technique (refer to Table 8.2).

Table 8.3 shows the mean values of achieved new product forecasting accuracy across the six types of new products (accuracy data were collected by asking respondents to indicate the average forecast accuracy achieved one year after launch and the typical forecast time horizons across the six types of new products). A total of 49 companies provided data on their new product forecast accuracies. The overall average accuracy across the six types of new products was 58 percent, with cost reductions generally 72 percent accurate; product improvement forecasts 65 percent accurate; line extension forecasts 63 percent accurate; market extension forecasts 54 percent accurate; new category entry (new-to-the-company) forecasts 47 percent; and new-to-the-world products 40 percent accurate (refer to Table 8.3).

The nature of these accuracies suggests that newer markets are more troublesome to forecast (i.e., market extensions, new category entries, and new-to-the-world products), than those situations where a current market is being served (i.e., cost reductions, product improvements, line extensions). While it may seem intuitive, these results suggest that it is not the product/technology, but rather the market/customer-base that impacts new product forecast accuracy.

The overall average forecast time horizon for these forecasts is approximately twenty-six months. As shown in Table 8.3, the average time horizons for cost reductions, product improvements, line extensions, and market extensions were below this average (twenty-one months, twenty months, twenty-one months, and twenty-four months, respectively), while the average time horizons for new category entries and new-to-the-world products were above this average (thirty-five months and thirty-six months, respectively). These results suggest that forecasts for new category entries and new-to-the-world products are characteristically longer-term in nature, and correspondingly, more strategic in nature than forecasts for the other types of new products.

Respondents also were asked about their satisfaction with their company's new product forecasting process using a five-point Likert scale. Of the 150 who responded to the question, 8 percent were "very dissatisfied" with their new product forecasting process, 45 percent were "dissatisfied," 27 percent were neutral, 19 percent were "satisfied," and only 1 percent of respondents were "very satisfied" with their new product forecasting process. Because more than half of companies surveyed were dissatisfied with their new product forecasting process, it would appear that new product forecasting is an area in need of improvement, and consequently, deserving of continued attention.

Table 8.4

Examining the Forecast Accuracy–Satisfaction Relationship

	Pearson correlation between accuracy and satisfaction
Cost reductions ($n = 29$)	.419*
Product improvements ($n = 45$)	.230
Line extensions ($n = 45$)	.302*
Market extensions ($n = 42$)	.346*
New category entries (new-to-the-company) ($n = 30$)	.367*
New-to-the-world ($n = 39$)	.257

Satisfaction level	Overall average accuracy			
	First quartile (up to 42.92% overall accuracy)	Second quartile (42.92% to 60% overall accuracy)	Third quartile (60% to 75% overall accuracy)	Fourth quartile (75% and better overall accuracy)
Very dissatisfied	8.3%			
Dissatisfied	58.3%	64.3%	38.5%	30%
Neutral	33.3%	28.6%	15.4%	20%
Satisfied			46.2%	50%
Very satisfied		7.1%		
Count	12	14	13	10

Notes:
* = $p < .05$
n = sample size
Spearman Correlation between accuracy and satisfaction = .409 ($p < .01$)
Gamma = .477 ($p < .01$)

A possible relationship between accuracy and satisfaction was examined due to the premise that companies achieving better new product forecast accuracy would likely be more satisfied with the new product forecasting process (Kahn and Mentzer 1994). Analysis revealed statistically significant ($p < .05$) correlational relationships between satisfaction and achieved forecast accuracy across four of the six types of new products, and between satisfaction and overall forecast accuracy ($p < .01$). Such results support the premise of an accuracy–satisfaction relationship (see Table 8.4), but because the magnitudes of each correlation are below .50, it would appear that accuracy explains less than 25 percent of satisfaction's variance, and vice versa. Thus, forecast accuracy may be a driver of satisfaction, but it is not the only driver; conversely, satisfaction may be considered a corresponding measure of forecast accuracy, but it should not be considered an equivalent measure.

Further analysis investigated how different departments' involvement, use of various techniques, and the number of techniques used might correlate to higher forecast accuracy or greater satisfaction with the new product forecasting process. Due to the finding of a significant correlation between accuracy and satisfaction, partial correlations were employed to examine each respective variable's relationship with accuracy, while controlling for satisfaction, and with satisfaction, while controlling for accuracy (a partial correlation is an index of the proportional increase in explained variance between two variables, holding all remaining variables constant).

Overall, these results fail to show a general linkage relating involvement of any particular department, use of any particular technique, or the number of techniques used with accuracy or satisfaction across the six types of new products. Although various statistically significant individual findings were identified, the large number of nonsignificant findings suggests that these variables alone are not drivers of new product forecast accuracy or satisfaction (see Tables 8.5 and 8.6). This counters previous research, which has suggested that the greater the number of techniques used will lead to higher forecast accuracy. Based on the results, it would appear that simply increasing various departments' involvement, focusing on particular technique, or increasing the number of techniques used will not likely translate into a more accurate or a more satisfying new product forecasting effort.

Examining Differences Between Consumer and Industrial Firms

Further analyses segmented study data to compare practices of strictly consumer versus strictly industrial (business-to-business) firms. Several statistically significant differences were found, but the most striking difference was industrial firms having longer time horizons for new product forecasts than consumer firms. On average, industrial firms have a thirty-four month forecast horizon versus an eighteen-month horizon in the case of consumer firms. It may be that the contractual nature of industrial relationships and capacity issues surrounding the larger volumes associated with industrial markets orients, if not mandates, an industrial firm to pursue longer-range forecasting.

Another difference is a preference by industrial firms to use the sales

Table 8.5

Partial Correlations Between Technique Use, Accuracy, and Satisfaction

Forecasting technique (in order of most-used to least-used)	CR (n = 21) Acc	Sat	PI (n = 38) Acc	Sat	LE (n = 36) Acc	Sat	ME (n = 33) Acc	Sat	NCE (n = 23) Acc	Sat	NTW (n = 31) Acc	Sat
Customer/market research	**.51**	.15	.07	.03	.26	-.23	.16	.17	**.47**	-.09	.26	-.12
Jury of executive opinion	-.01	-.11	.02	**-.33**	.01	**-.28**	-.06	-.27	.11	-.05	**.30**	-.20
Sales force composite	-.29	-.06	-.05	-.20	-.09	**-.29**	-.02	-.17	.01	-.16	-.14	-.14
Looks-like analysis	-.10	**-.37**	-.14	-.19	-.10	-.13	-.16	-.16	-.07	-.50	-.02	-.17
Trend line analysis	-.19	-.19	-.25	-.18	.04	-.25	-.12	-.20	.11	.09	.06	-.05
Moving average	-.20	.03	-.10	-.13	.01	-.14	.13	-.24	**.34**	-.32	**.33**	-.26
Scenario analysis	-.12	.13	-.13	-.05	-.16	.04	-.20	-.03	-.21	.02	**-.33**	-.01
Exponential smoothing techniques	-.26	-.13	-.15	.03	-.08	.04	.07	-.11	-.02	-.14	.03	-.12
Experience curves	.11	-.22	.09	.15	.06	.20	.04	.22	.22	.02	.09	.23
Market analysis model (incl. ATAR model)	n/a	n/a	.08	.07	.07	.21	.10	.22	.22	.06	-.03	-.08
Delphi method	-.13	-.17	-.16	-.12	-.02	-.13	-.12	.01	-.05	-.20	-.14	-.10
Linear regression	.11	.09	-.15	**.34**	-.24	.22	.10	.22	n/a	n/a	-.20	-.06
Decision trees	.18	-.08	-.14	-.14	-.17	.14	.07	.03	.10	.07	-.10	.19
Simulation	n/a	n/a	-.25	.11	**-.36**	.18	-.14	.27	.18	.18	.22	.11
Expert systems	.04	.30	-.10	.14	.15	.04	.28	.15	n/a	n/a	-.20	-.06

Other	.04	.30	n/a	n/a	n/a	n/a	n/a	n/a	-.29	-.07	n/a	n/a
Nonlinear regression	n/a	n/a	n/a	n/a	-.06	-.09	.21	.03	.24	.21	.13	.11
Diffusion models	n/a	n/a	.02	.22	-.01	.23	n/a	n/a	n/a	n/a	n/a	n/a
Precursor curves (correlation method)	n/a	n/a	-.11	.08	.12	.02	-.06	.09	n/a	n/a	n/a	n/a
Box-Jenkins techniques (ARMA/ARIMA)	n/a	n/a	n/a	n/a	n/a	n/a	n/a	n/a	n/a	n/a	n/a	n/a

Notes:

Acc = partial correlation with accuracy, controlling for satisfaction;

Sat = partial correlation with satisfaction, controlling for accuracy;

CR = cost reductions: reduced cost or price versions of the product for the existing market;

PI = product improvements: new, improved versions of existing products/services, targeted to the current market;

LE = line extensions: incremental innovations added to existing product lines and targeted to the current market;

ME = market extensions: taking existing products/services to new markets;

NCE = new category entries: new-to-the-company product and new-to-the-company market, but not new to the general market;

NTW = new-to-the-world products: radically different products/services versus current offerings and markets served.

Note that bold items are statistically different at $p < .10$.

n = sample size

Table 8.6

Partial Correlations Between Number of Techniques Used, Accuracy, and Satisfaction

Type of new product	Partial correlation between accuracy and number of techniques used	Partial correlation between satisfaction and number of techniques used
Cost reductions ($n = 21$)	−.06	−.19
Product improvements ($n = 38$)	−.26	−.16
Line extensions ($n = 36$)	−.07	−.20
Market extensions ($n = 33$)	−.00	−.08
New category entries ($n = 23$)		
(new-to-the-company)	.29	−.24
New-to-the-world ($n = 31$)	.09	−.17

Notes:
n = Sample size
None of the above items were statistically different at $p < .10$.

force composite method for forecasting product improvements, line extensions, and market extensions. This corresponds to research that shows the popularity of sales-based forecasts in the case of industrial firms (Mentzer and Kahn 1995). It therefore would appear that industrial firms rely more on their sales forces than consumer firms to derive forecasts, regardless of whether such forecasts concern existing or new products. Refer to Table 8.7.

Benchmark Study Conclusions

These benchmarking study results offer the following insights into practices related to new product forecasting:

- Almost two-thirds of companies have the marketing department responsible for the new product forecasting effort; even if not responsible, the marketing department is heavily involved in the new product forecasting effort.
- Sales, sales forecasting, and market research are other departments that appear to have an appreciable level of involvement in the new product forecasting effort.
- There is a preference toward qualitative forecasting techniques and

market research (which may be qualitative or quantitative) when forecasting new products. In fact, a majority of companies indicated using customer/market research techniques to forecast new products.

- Companies appear to apply techniques equally across the different types of new products.
- Companies typically use more than one new product forecasting technique—on average, two to four forecasting techniques. However, results suggest that the greater the number of techniques used does not simply lead to higher new product forecast accuracy or greater satisfaction with the new product forecasting process.
- One should expect higher forecast accuracy with cost reductions and product improvements than new-to-the-world products. Overall, the average forecast accuracy across all types of new products is 58 percent.
- Compared to consumer firms, industrial firms have longer forecast time horizons and rely more on the sales force for new product forecasting.

The exploratory nature of the PDMA new product forecasting benchmarking study warrants continued work to confirm its results, and delineate ways to improve the new product forecasting effort. Such process improvement is certainly needed given that the overall accuracy of new product forecasts is 58 percent. Indeed, the level of achieved forecast accuracy suggests that companies are either making approximately twice as much inventory as they need, or companies are meeting only half of the actual demand for a new product. Any efforts to improve accuracy can serve to improve new product success and business performance, that is, inventory and customer service, which correspond to a direct bottom-line impact. Satisfaction also may have a relationship with new product success and business performance, but maybe not as clear a relationship as forecast accuracy. Results also show customer/market research, which actually encompasses a variety of approaches, to be the most popular new product forecasting technique. One possible explanation for such "popularity" is a perception that this technique may be important to new product forecasting success (although the empirical results failed to show that use of customer/market research correlates to higher forecast accuracy or greater satisfaction).

The overall conclusion of the PDMA benchmarking study is that new

Table 8.7

Statistically Significant Differences Between Consumer and Industrial Firms

Characteristic	Statistical differences ($p < .10$)
Department responsibility	• Finance is responsible for new product forecasting in 10% of consumer firms versus 0% of industrial firms [$p < .05$] • R&D is responsible for new product forecasting in 0% of consumer firms versus 7% of industrial firms [$p < .05$]
Average level of involvement	• R&D is more involved in new product forecasting in the case of industrial firms (mean = 3.58, sd = 1.23) versus consumer firms (mean = 2.41, sd = 1.46) [$p < .05$]
Technique usage	• 32% of industrial firms use experience curves to forecast cost reductions versus 0% of consumer firms [$p < .05$] • 19% of industrial firms use experience curves to forecast product improvements versus 6% of consumer firms [$p < .05$] • 51% of industrial firms use the sales force composite method to forecast product improvements versus 28% of consumer firms [$p < .05$] • 11% of consumer firms use simulation to forecast product improvements versus 2% of industrial firms [$p < .10$] • 10% of industrial firms use expert systems to forecast line extensions versus 0% of consumer firms [$p < .05$] • 50% of industrial firms use jury of executive opinion to forecast line extensions versus 29% of consumer firms [$p < .05$] • 62% of industrial firms use the sales force composite method to forecast line extensions versus 29% of consumer firms [$p < .05$] • 9% of industrial firms use expert systems to forecast market extensions versus 0% of consumer firms [$p < .05$] • 53% of industrial firms use the sales force composite method to forecast market extensions versus 29% of consumer firms [$p < .05$] • 12% of industrial firms use experience curves to forecast new-to-the-world products versus 2% of consumer firms [$p < .10$] • 19% of consumer firms use trend line analysis to forecast new-to-the-world products versus 5% of industrial firms [$p < .10$]

Forecast accuracy	No statistical differences revealed

Time horizon   • Industrial firms have a longer forecast time horizon across all types of new products than consumer firms (all statistically significant at $p < .05$, except line extension which is statistically significant at $p < .10$):

Type of new product	Consumer firms	Industrial firms
Cost reduction	13.09 months	24.60 months
	($s = 6.47$, $n = 11$)	($s = 16.62$, $n = 20$)
Product improvement	16.08	23.53
	($s = 12.70$, $n = 49$)	($s = 17.68$, $n = 32$)
Line extension	17.85	25.88
	($s = 19.59$, $n = 47$)	($s = 17.27$, $n = 32$)
Market extension	16.58	31.88
	($s = 13.62$, $n = 44$)	($s = 21.74$, $n = 32$)
New category entry	16.54	48.29
	($s = 8.65$, $n = 13$)	($s = 41.76$, $n = 21$)
New-to-the-world	24.51	51.15
	($s = 26.81$, $n = 45$)	($s = 44.03$, $n = 33$)

Notes:
Differences in percent for the areas of Department Responsibility and Technique Usage were evaluated using z-tests.

Differences in numbers for the areas of Average Level of Involvement, Forecast Accuracy, and Time Horizon were evaluated using t-tests.

n = sample size
s = standard deviation

product forecasting should be conceived of as more than just applying a forecasting technique and measuring the accuracy of that technique. The findings concerning the use of multiple techniques and the involvement of multiple departments with the goal to derive a sales estimate of what is most likely to occur exemplify that new product forecasting inherently reflects process characteristics. New product forecasting should therefore be viewed from the broader process perspective.

Final Observations

Experience in working with companies has augmented these benchmarking study conclusions. Here are additional observations and prescriptions regarding an applied approach toward new product forecasting.

- First, there is no silver bullet when it comes to new product forecasting. There are multiple techniques and ways to derive a forecast. Some are better than others, but there is no one, perfect forecasting technique out there. The reality is that all new product forecasts are wrong. The issue is deriving meaningful forecasts that can be readily applied across the company. Some may see this as a disappointment, but it is a steadfast reality of new product forecasting.
- Second, forecasting success is a result of data, experience, a cooperative relationship with marketing, cross-functional communication, business knowledge, and being connected to the customer. Reappraisal and verification of forecasting assumptions can only come about because of interaction across functional departments. Each department can bring incremental data and knowledge about the marketplace and technology capabilities that, in aggregate, benefit the overall learning process superimposed over the new product forecasting process.
- Third, participation of analytical business functions like market research and sales forecasting correlate to a more accurate, satisfying forecast. Judgmental techniques are popular and a necessary part of new product forecasting, but judgment alone is not sufficient. Analysis of past data, surrogate products, and consumer responsiveness to marketing variables offer "harder" data on which to base new product decisions. Simply relying on anecdotal evidence and gut feel, in lieu of analysis, can lead management decisions astray, especially when the data and information exists and can be readily analyzed.
- Fourth, new product forecasting requires reconciliation of multiple techniques based on judgment and analytical skills. However, the greater the number of techniques used does not simply increase new product forecast accuracy nor satisfaction with the new product forecasting process. Having multiple forecasts allows for the triangulation of forecasts and rationales that underlie the new product forecast. In fact, there is a benefit in having multiple, distinct new product forecasts because it forces robust discussion over the assumptions and issues that underlie the new product, likely resulting in more thoughtful determination of the new product forecast.
- Fifth, think in terms of ranges, not specific numbers. Those companies that I would consider best practice realize the new product

forecasts will be wrong. Yet, they understand that bounding the new product forecast between pessimistic and optimistic ranges allows for better launch planning and financial target setting. Those companies fixated on point forecasts become too preoccupied in hitting a "number." Better companies realize that new product forecasting is *not* about hitting a number; rather, it is about being market responsive and superior at providing customer service, which range forecasting will allow.

Implications for Your Company's New Product Forecasting Process

Several questions are posed to frame one's evaluation of their company's new product forecasting process. While there are no right or wrong answers, these questions attune discussion and thinking to the issues that abound during new product forecasting. The ability to readily generate an answer to each of the following questions is an indicator that at least the respective company has an applied approach for new product forecasting, albeit it may need tuning.

- What is the new product forecasting objective?
- Given this objective, what should be forecast?
- What assumptions can be used to forecast a respective new product?
- How can/should these assumptions be operationalized?
- What assumptions appear to be common across new products forecasts?
- What prelaunch data sources are available?
- What assumptions/variables can and should be tracked?
- How can these variables be tracked, both prelaunch and postlaunch?
- What is the appropriate process and how can it be successfully linked to the Sales and Operations Planning (S&OP) process?

Answering these questions should help provide greater understanding of the new product forecasting environment. Moreover, answering these questions should provoke new thinking about the uniqueness, nuances, and distinct requirements of new product forecasting versus regular sales forecasting in the course of designing, implementing, and monitoring a new product forecasting process. Best wishes for successful and meaningful new product forecasting.

Key Concepts

New Product Forecasting Practices
New Product Forecast Accuracy
Prescriptions for Applied New Product Forecasting

Discussion Questions

1. Which new product forecasting technique(s) are popular?
2. Should a company use more than one technique when forecasting new products? Why or why not?
3. What is the nature of forecast accuracy across the different types
   of new products?
4. Do consumer and industrial goods firms differ with regard to
   new product forecasting?
5. What is range forecasting versus point forecasting? Which one
   is recommended for new product forecasting?

References

Adams-Bigelow, Marjorie E. (2004). "First Results from the 2003 Comparative Performance Assessment Study (CPAS)." In the *PDMA Handbook of New Product Development* (2nd ed.), ed. Kenneth B. Kahn, 546–66. Hoboken, NJ: Wiley.

American Marketing Association. (2000). *Preference Structure Measurement: Conjoint Analysis and Related Techniques: A Guide for Designing and Interpreting Conjoint Studies.* 2nd ed. New York: Intelliquest.

Armstrong, J. Scott. (1996). "Comment on William B. Gartner and Robert J. Thomas, 1993, Factors Affecting New Product Forecasting Accuracy in New Firms." *International Journal of Forecasting* 12 (2): 321–22.

Bayus, Barry L. (1987). "Forecasting Sales of New Contingent Products: An Application to the Compact Disc Market." *Journal of Product Innovation Management* 4 (4): 243–55.

BBC News. "Burger Giant Plans Clothing Range." http://newswww.bbc.net.uk/2/hi/business/3567529.stm.

Beardsley, George, and Edwin Mansfield. (1978). "A Note on the Accuracy of Industrial Forecasts of the Profitability of New Products and Processes." *Journal of Business* 51 (1): 127–35.

Chase, Richard B., and Nicholas J. Aquilano. (1985). *Production and Operations Management: A Life Cycle Approach.* Homewood, IL: Irwin.

Choffray, Jean-Marie, and Gary L. Lilien. (1986). "A Decision Support System for Evaluating Sales Prospects and Launch Strategies for New Products." *Industrial Marketing Management* 15 (1): 75–85.

Clemen, Robert T. (1997). *Making Hard Decisions: An Introduction to Decision Analysis.* Belmont, CA: Duxbury Press.

Cooper, Robert G. (1993). *Winning at New Products.* Reading, MA: Addison-Wesley.

Cooper, Robert G., Scott J. Edgett, and Elko J. Kleinschmidt. (1998). *Portfolio Management for New Products.* Reading, MA: Addison-Wesley.

Crawford, Merle C., and C. Anthony Di Benedetto. (2000). *New Products Management.* 6th ed. Boston: Irwin McGraw-Hill.

———. (2003). *New Products Management.* 7th ed. Boston: McGraw-Hill Irwin.

Dolan, Robert J. (1990). *Conjoint Analysis: A Manager's Guide.* Harvard Business School Case 590-059. Boston: Harvard Business School Press.

Food Week Magazine. (2004). "Gillette Taps New Market."

Gartner, William B., and Robert J. Thomas. (1993). "Factors Affecting New Product Forecasting Accuracy in New Firms." *Journal of Product Innovation Management* 10 (1): 35–52.

General Mills.com, Lucky Charm's website, www.generalmills.com/corporate/brands/product.aspx?catID=69#.

Goldner, Peter N., and Gerard J. Tellis. (1998). "Beyond Diffusion: An Affordability Model of the Growth of New Consumer Durables." *Journal of Forecasting* 17 (3–4): 259–80.

Hair, Joseph F., Jr., Rolph E. Anderson, Ronald L. Tatham, and William C. Black. (1998). *Multivariate Data Analysis,* 4th ed. New York: Macmillan.

Hardie, Burce G.S., Peter S. Fader, and Michael Wisniewski. (1998). "An Empirical Comparison of New Product Trial Forecasting Models." *Journal of Forecasting* 17 (3–4): 207–27.

Hauser, John R., and Don Clausing. (1988). "House of Quality." *Harvard Business Review* 66 (3): 63–73.

Heskett, James. (1976). *Marketing.* New York: MacMillan.

Jain, Dipak, Vijay Mahajan, and Eitan Muller. (1995). "An Approach for Determining Optimal Product Sampling for the Diffusion of a New Product." *Journal of Product Innovation Management* 12 (2): 124–35.

Kahn, Kenneth B. (2000). *Product Planning Essentials.* Thousand Oaks, CA: Sage.

———. (2002). "An Exploratory Investigation of New Product Forecasting Practices." *Journal of Product Innovation Management* 19 (2): 133–43.

Kahn, Kenneth B., and John T. Mentzer. (1994). "Team-Based Forecasting." *Journal of Business Forecasting* 13 (2): 18–21.

Kalish, Shlomo. (1985). "A New Product Diffusion Model with Price, Advertising and Uncertainty." *Management Science* 31 (12): 1569–85.

Kalish, Shlomo, and Gary L. Lilien. (1986). "A Market Entry Timing Model for New Technologies." *Management Science* 32 (2): 194–205.

Kelloggs.com, Eggo website, www.kelloggs.com/brand/eggo/home.

Lattin, James M., and John H. Roberts. (1998). "Calibrating an Individual Level Diffusion Model Prior to Launch." Working paper, Graduate School of Business, Stanford University, October.

Lenk, Peter J., and Ambar Rao. (1990). "New Products from Old: Forecasting Product Adoption by Hierarchical Bayes Procedures." *Marketing Science* 9 (1): 42–57.

Lilien, Gary L., and Arvind Rangaswamy. (1998). *Marketing Engineering.* Reading, MA: Addison Wesley Longman.

Lilien, Gary, Arvind Rangaswamy, and Christophe Van den Bulte. (1999). *Diffusion Models: Managerial Applications and Software.* Report No. 7–1999. University Park, PA: Institute for the Study of Business Markets.

Lomax, Wendy, Kathy Hammond, Robert East, and Maria Clemente. (1997). "The Measurement of Cannibalization." *Journal of Product and Brand Management* 6 (1): 27–39.

Lynn, Gary S., Steven P. Schnaars, and Richard B. Skov. (1999). "Survey of New Product Forecasting Practices in Industrial High Technology and Low Technology Businesses." *Industrial Marketing Management* 28 (6): 565–71.

Mahajan, Vijay, and Robert A. Peterson. (1985). *Models for Innovative Diffusion.* Newbury Park, CA: Sage.

Mahajan, Vijay, and Jerry Y. Wind. (1986). *Innovation Diffusion Models of New Product Acceptance.* Cambridge, MA: Ballinger.

———. (1992). "New Product Models: Practice, Shortcomings, and Desired Improvements." *Journal of Product Innovation Management* 9 (2): 128–39.

Mahajan, Vijay, Eitan Muller, and Frank M. Bass. (1990). "New Product Diffusion Models in Marketing: A Review and Directions for Research." *Journal of Marketing* 54 (1): 1–26.

Mahajan, Vijay, Eitan Muller, and Yoram Wind. (2000). *New-Product Diffusion Models.* New York: Springer Publishing Company.

Makridakis, Spyros, Steven C. Wheelwright, and Victor E. McGee. (1983). *Forecasting: Methods and Applications.* 2nd ed. New York: Wiley.

Makridakis, Spyros G., Steven C. Wheelwright, and Rob J. Hyndman. (1997). *Forecasting: Methods and Applications* (3rd ed.). Hoboken, NJ: John Wiley and Sons.

Mason, Robert D., and Douglas A. Lind. (1996). *Statistical Techniques in Business and Economics.* 9th ed. Chicago: Irwin.

Mentzer, John T., and Carol B. Bienstock. (1998). *Sales Forecasting Management.* Thousand Oaks, CA: Sage.

Mentzer, John T., and Kenneth B. Kahn. (1995). "Forecasting Technique Familiarity, Satisfaction, Usage, and Application." *Journal of Forecasting* 14 (5): 465–76.

Mentzer, John T., Carol C. Bienstock, and Kenneth B. Kahn. (1999). "Benchmarking Sales Forecasting Management." *Business Horizons* 42 (3): 48–56.

Moore, Geoffrey A. (1995). *Crossing the Chasm: Marketing and Selling High-Tech Products to Mainstream Customers.* New York: Harper Business.

Morrison, Jeffrey. (1996). "How to Use Diffusion Models in New Product Forecasting." *Journal of Business Forecasting* 15 (Summer): 6–9.

———. (1999). "New-Product Forecasting." *PDMA Visions Magazine,* July 10.

Neter, John, Michael H. Kutner, Christopher J. Nachtsheim, and William Wasserman. (1996). *Applied Liner Regression Models.* 3rd ed. Chicago: Irwin.

Ozer, Muammer. (1999). "A Survey of New Product Evaluation Models." *Journal of Product Innovation Management* 16 (1): 77–94.

Pullman, Madeleine E., William L. Moore, and Don G. Wardell. (2002). "A Comparison of Quality Function Deployment and Conjoint Analysis in New Product Design." *Journal of Product Innovation Management* 19 (5): 354–64.

Quelch, John A., and John Teopaco. (1986). *General Mills, Inc.: Yoplait Custard-Style Yogurt (B).* Harvard Business School Case 586-088. Boston: Harvard Business School Press.

Ram, Sundaresan, and Sudha Ram. (1996). "Validation of Expert Systems for Innovation Management: Issues, Methodology, and Empirical Assessment." *Journal of Product Innovation Management* 13 (1): 53–68.

Rao, Sanjay-Kumar. (1985). "An Empirical Comparison of Sales Forecasting Models." *Journal of Product Innovation Management* 2 (4): 232–42.

Rogers, Everett M. (1995). *Diffusion of Innovations.* 4th ed. New York: Free Press.

Saunders, John. (1985). "New Product Forecasting in the UK." *The Quarterly Review of Marketing* (Spring): 1–11.

Sawhney, Mohan, and Jehoshua Eliashberg. (1996). "A Parsimonious Model for Forecasting Gross Box Office Revenues of Motion Pictures." *Marketing Science* 15 (2): 113–31.

Shelley, Charles J., and David R. Wheeler. (1991). "New Product Forecasting Horizons and Accuracy." *Review of Business* 12 (4): 13–18.

Stein, Ellen, and Marco Iansiti. (1995). *Understanding Customer Needs*. HBS Case Note No. 9–695–051. Boston: Harvard Business School Press.

Sultan, Fareena, John U. Farley, and Donald R. Lehmann. (1990). "A Meta Analysis of Applications of Diffusion Models." *Journal of Marketing Research*. 27 (1): 70–77.

Thomas, Robert J. (1985). "Estimating Market Growth for New Products: An Analogical Diffusion Model Approach." *Journal of Product Innovation Management* 2 (1): 45–55.

———. (1993). *New Product Development: Managing and Forecasting for Strategic Success*. New York: Wiley.

Tull, D.S. (1967). "The Relationship of Actual and Predicted Sales in New Product Introductions." *Journal of Business* 40: 233–50.

Urban, Glen L., and John R. Hauser. (1993). *Design and Marketing of New Products*. 2nd ed. Englewood Cliffs, NJ: Prentice Hall.

von Hippel, Eric. (1988). *The Sources of Innovation*. New York: Oxford University Press.

Wallace, Thomas F. (1999). *Sales & Operations Planning: The How-to Handbook*. Cincinnati, OH: T. F. Wallace.

Weida, Nancy C., Ronny Richardson, and Andrew Vazonyi. (2001). *Operations Analysis Using Microsoft Excel*. Pacific Grove, CA: Duxbury.

Wind, Yoram, Vijay Mahajan, and Richard N. Cardozo. (1981). *New-Product Forecasting: Models and Applications*. Lexington, MA: Lexington Books.

Wyndham.com. (2004). "Wyndham Unleashes Another Hotel Industry First: Affordable Mini-Bars." www.wyndham.com/corporate/pressreleases/pressreleasedetail/main .wnt?ReleaseID=520405.

Index

Kenneth B. Kahn (BIE, Georgia Institute of Technology; MSIE, Virginia Polytechnic Institute and State University; Ph.D. in Marketing, Virginia Polytechnic Institute and State University) is a tenured Associate Professor of Marketing and a College of Business Administration Reagan Scholar in the Department of Marketing and Logistics at the University of Tennessee. His teaching and research interests concern product development, product management, and forecasting of existing and new products. He has published in a variety of journals, including the *Journal of Product Innovation Management, Journal of Business Research, Journal of Forecasting, Journal of Business Forecasting, Marketing Management,* and *R&D Management.* He is the author of the book *Product Planning Essentials* and editor of the *PDMA Handbook on New Product Development,* 2nd edition.

Dr. Kahn is cofounding Director of the University of Tennessee's Sales Forecasting Management Forum, which specializes in education and research involving market analysis and sales forecasting. He is also the current Vice President of Publications for the Product Development and Management Association (www.pdma.org). Prior to joining the faculty at the University of Tennessee, Dr. Kahn was Director of Georgia Tech's Marketing Analysis Laboratory and cofounder of Georgia Tech's Collaborative Product Development Laboratory, both of which conducted corporate-sponsored research.

Dr. Kahn's industrial experience includes serving as an industrial engineer and project engineer for the Weyerhaeuser Company and a manufacturing engineer for Respironics, Inc. He has consulted with and facilitated benchmarking sessions with numerous companies, including 3M, Acco Brands, Amgen, Biolab, Borden, Cargill, Cheps USA, Ciba Specialty Chemicals, Coca-Cola, Corning, Enterasys Networks, Gillette, Hanes/L'eggs, Hewlett-Packard, Lifescan, Mary Kay Cosmetics, McNeil Consumer Healthcare, Miller Brewing Company, Moen, Motorola, Mrs. Smith's Bakeries, Nabisco, Pharmavite, Schering-Plough, SmithKline Beecham, Springs Industries, Symbol Technologies, Tropicana, Unilever, and Xerox.